LOS ANGELES REVIEW OF BOOKS

NO. 18 QUARTERLY JOURNAL: GENIUS

COVER ART: KERRY JAMES MARSHALL

front: *PORTRAIT OF A CURATOR (IN MEMORY OF BERYL WRIGHT)*, 2009, ACRYLIC ON PVC, 30 7/8 X 24 7/8 X 1 7/8 INCHES, PENNY PRITZKER AND BRYAN TRAUBERT COLLECTION © KERRY JAMES MARSHALL / COURTESY OF THE ARTIST AND JACK SHAINMAN GALLERY, NEW YORK

back: *UNTITLED (STUDIO)*, 2014, ACRYLIC ON PVC PANEL 83 ½ X 118 7/8 INCHES / COURTESY THE ARTIST AND DAVID ZWIRNER, LONDON

The Los Angeles Review of Books is a 501(c)(3) nonprofit organization. The *LARB Quarterly Journal* is published quarterly by the Los Angeles Review of Books, 6671 Sunset Blvd., Suite 1521, Los Angeles, CA 90028. Submissions for the *Journal* can be emailed to EDITORIAL@LAREVIEWOFBOOKS.ORG. Visit our website at WWW.LAREVIEWOFBOOKS.ORG.

The *LARB Quarterly Journal* is a premium of the LARB Membership Program. Annual subscriptions are available. Go to WWW.LAREVIEWOFBOOKS.ORG/MEMBERSHIP for more information or email MEMBERSHIP@LAREVIEWOFBOOKS.ORG.

Distribution through Publishers Group West. If you are a retailer and would like to order the *LARB Quarterly Journal*, call 800-788-3123 or email orderentry@perseusbooks.com.

To place an ad in the *LARB Quarterly Journal*, email ADSALES@LAREVIEWOFBOOKS.ORG.

CONTENTS

NO. 18 QUARTERLY JOURNAL: GENIUS

essays

17 DISTRIBUTED GENIUS
by Johanna Drucker

38 THE RISE AND FALL OF THE FILOSOFESSA
by Massimo Mazzotti

74 A SPLENDID HISTORY: HENRY LOUIS GATES JR. ON AFRICA'S ANCIENT CIVILIZATIONS
by Scott Timberg

105 MARTYR AT THE PICNIC TABLE
by Aaron Robertson

129 NEWS FROM HOME
by Sara Jaffe

138 GENIUS AND DAEMON
by AE Stallings

fiction

22 IN THE BEGINNING
by Isaac Bashevis Singer
translated by David Stromberg

53 YOUTUBE COMMENT #2 TO BJÖRK...
by Yxta Maya Murray

80 BEHIND THE MOON
by Anosh Irani

115 THE PRINCIPAL'S ASHES
by Jac Jemc

133 UNA GOCCIA
by Dino Buzatti
translated by Zoë Slutzky

poetry

34 EXCERPTS FROM THE *KINGDOM OF SURFACES*
by Sally Wen Mao

70 MARINA IN NERVI
by David Yezzi

100 SAM'S DREAM
by Jorie Graham

120 GRADUS AD PARNASSUM
by Rachel Hadas

124 TWO POEMS
by Joshua Bennett

140 VIVIAN MAIER CONSIDERS HEAVEN FROM A BENCH IN ROGERS BEACH PARK CHICAGO
by Shane McCrae

shorts

32 MORE LIKE YOU
by Sloane Crosley

64 THE FAMILY GENIUSES
by Zeynep Kayhan

96 THE WRONG STUFF
by Helen DeWitt

122 LISA BONET
by Venita Blackburn

136 BARE IN MIND
by Hilary Leichter

144 A DEFINITION OF GENIUS
by Paul LaFarge

Luchita Hurtado, Untitled (Self-portrait), c. 1968, oil on linen, 32 1/2 x 26 3/4 inches
Courtesy the artist and Park View/Paul Soto Los Angeles and Brussels. Photo: Jeff Mclane

Gala Porras-Kim, *31 west Mexico ceramics from LACMA collection: Jalisco Index*, 2017, graphite, colored pencil, marker, ink on paper, artist's frame, 73 x 73 x 3 inches / Courtesy the artist and Commonwealth and Council. Photo: Ruben Diaz

Dear Reader,

I sometimes imagine genius as a very fast moving body of water. People naturally slip in and out but it's impossible to jump in. Or it's like living in a house, where I'm generally free to wander at will, but the upper floors are boarded up. I know there are people up there, I can hear them, but who knows how they got upstairs, it looks pretty locked to me. This isn't something to take personally — you either have access or you don't. And besides, I can't think of a more appropriate application for that Groucho Marx quote: genius is exactly the kind of club I would resign from if it ever accepted a person like me as a member.

But why do I think of genius as necessarily exclusionary? This says something about me, but it must also say something about the word. As Jameson (a genius) once wrote, "Always historicize." He was referring to another Marx altogether but this quote also seems apt. Genius is after all, a term that can be taken in a social, historical, and yes, material context. This issue of the *Los Angeles Review of Books Quarterly Journal* is dedicated to an examination of that tricky word. There have been, unequivocally, more recognized male geniuses than female, though as Massimo Mazzotti points out in his essay on the *filosofessa*, there was a brief period in 18th century Italy where the genius of little girls was fostered. Johanna Drucker makes the case for understanding the term in a broader sense — not as something confined to individuals but distributed widely through the world, in systems and organisms. Helen DeWitt talks about the ways in which publishing still defines what literature is or isn't. Yxta Maya Murray writes about Björk, motherhood, the possible destruction and synergy involved in creation. You will also see many pieces that play with the word, poke fun at it, and redefine it in their own terms.

We also have works in this issue by poets, writers and artists that we'd like to celebrate in the context of genius. Whatever we think of the term, we can at least use it as an acknowledgement of extraordinary accomplishment.

This issue isn't about pushing anyone out of those upper floors, it is more about investigating the rules of membership. Or, to put genius back in Marxist terms: it is perhaps, a way of giving more people the opportunity to resign.

Medaya
Editor, Quarterly Journal

Kerry James Marshall, *Past Times*, 1997, acrylic and collage on canvas, 114 x 156 inches
Courtesy Metropolitan Pier and Exposition Authority, McCormick Place Art Collection, photo by Nathan Keay © MCA Chicago

with heart and will

Gala Porras-Kim, *Three joined acrobats vessel*, 2017, graphite, Flashe paint on paper, artist's frame, 25.75 x 18.5 x 1.5 inches / Courtesy the artist and Commonwealth and Council. Photo: Ruben Diaz

DISTRIBUTED GENIUS

JOHANNA DRUCKER

Genius, conceived as innate spirit — the presence of the divine within each individual — has in the contemporary age become associated with uniqueness and distinction. In common conception, genius is a gift that bestows original power and inspired capacity. We ascribe rarity to the concept, unlike the ancients, who saw it as the general divinity of the world present within us all and each individually. We consider genius the most extreme form of exceptionalism. Our genius pantheon is populated by individuals whose accomplishments in science, the arts, philosophy, or politics seem to have been the outcome of inspirations so original that they transcend the given order and produce previously un-thought of results. Albert Einstein, Hildegard of Bingen, Wolfgang Amadeus Mozart, Marie Curie, Leonardo da Vinci, Sojourner Truth, John Locke — we can easily conjure the names. Human beings — they exemplify exceptionalism. Their *apartness*, their distinctiveness, becomes an identifying feature of their capability.

This definition of genius sentences us to a paradigm of individualism and human exceptionalism in which only *homo sapiens* can demonstrate the properties of creative imagination and only as autonomously conceived individuals. Why should this be the case? And might there be a different way to think about the concept of genius in aggregate terms or across a distributed field rather than distinction and differentiation? If we think within and outside of the human species, is there a way that emergent sentience and collective agency can arise from — *and as* — another kind of innate spirit?

Our narcissism blinds us to the genius of the world — its varieties of sentience and agency. We do not see the creative and generative forces of collective, aggregate, holistic forms of identity. These forces may be present in the physical world, like the "vibrant matter" referenced by Jane Bennett in a book of the same title or the universe that "meets us halfway" in the words of Karen Barad. These forms of identity certainly include aggregate life forms, but they also extend to facets of human social activity (for purposes of this short polemic, only animate species are considered as cases of distributed intelligence). This consideration can change the way we understand the human cultural condition — our condition — now. It may also lend the question some urgency because the concept of genius as currently conceived is an obstacle to thinking beyond the individual as a social unit and as a single, independent participant in cultural processes.

Our paradigm of sentience is part of the reason we think about genius in this particular way. We are wedded to the myth of the bounded person, of the autonomous individual. We conceive of sentience as interior to oneself, as if awareness were "inside" of us. We think of it as being transacted across the evident portals and thresholds of exchange. Our eyes, tongues, language, gesture, modes of communication are considered the mechanical and perceptual means of engaging in social modes. The "I" that relates to other living systems — "them" — is understood as separate and apart and we often eschew any recognition of the distributed forces that work so evidently within these other systems. We ignore therefore the implications of these processes of distributed effect. We allow mechanical paradigms, the Newtonian physics of the social world, to prevail — as if quantum theory and complex systems, or even the power of electromagnetism, ultraviolet light, the effects of neutrinos, shockwaves, the persuasiveness of pheromones, and other demonstrably present factors did not ignore those mythic boundaries of autonomous self-hood. We constantly pretend our isolation, as if we were not part of holistically effective and affective systems. We pretend despite so much evidence to the contrary. Think for example, about social media. If we think of genius as the spirit of the larger world, divine or not, that manifests itself through us, then social media demonstrates daily the rampant and unfettered force of emergent and distributed genius. It's a matter of reframing the concept: genius, not as differentiation and distinction, but a wide, distributed, sentient system.

Our focus on exceptionalism keeps us from observing and reckoning with these issues in the human species, but we are still confronted with and confounded by phenomena in the wider world. Take this one incident: in 2001 a red rain fell in Kerala, India — blood red. The droplets abounded in life forms that at first seemed unlike any on earth. These were microorganisms capable of surviving the extreme temperatures and vacuum void of interstellar space. Speculation went wild. Fringe groups claimed alien sources, imagining a repeat performance of what might have happened 3.8 billion or so years ago when the archaea, meteor-borne organisms, may have arrived on a young and still-forming earth (or, as others suggest, organic compounds first formed their affectionate bonds and hydrogen and carbon linked to each other in that boot-strapping effect that turned into terrestrial life). It turned out that the vivid color in that wild rain was caused by the spores of a widespread lichen, a hybrid offspring of a yearning algae and a sympathetic fungus. The algae and fungus covered a huge geographical area in Southeast Asia, and they were replicating with rapid enthusiasm. But for that rain to come down in a color dark as blood and across such a wide geographical expanse, these distributed colonies of lichen would have had to be in sync. They would have had to release their spores at the same moment — as in some completely coordinated simultaneous act of exhalation. This is statistically improbable and yet, it happened. As if the whole system were thinking feeling, acting, longing, coordinating as a single being that decided to act as one organism.

Swarm behaviors are usually understood as the coordinated actions of insect colonies, fungi, and large populations of unicellular organisms, acting in concert despite the lack of a designated lead, infrastructure of social hierarchy, or decision-making power. These behaviors still puzzle the scientific community. Often, science can only explain the processes of chemical communication or provide descriptions of complexity. It can catalogue the nuances in start conditions that otherwise unfold with non-linear consequences. But these are not explanations of causality, and we are faced with the profound question of how to account for these coordinated effects. We might also be left thinking about what it might mean to transfer these observations to the social world. Perhaps these ideas might help us explain the cultural realm of human behaviors, which might otherwise seem irrational and socially aberrant, especially when the illusion of rational enlightenment decorum is exposed for what it is.

When Roland Barthes and Michel Foucault each, differently, announced the demise of authorship half a century ago, and when Elias Canetti, decades earlier, sought explanations for the behavior of crowds, and when Theodor Adorno and Max Horkheimer struggled with the end of Enlightenment illusions — all were edging toward rethinking the understanding of the social production of texts, identity, behaviors, collective actions, and beliefs. Niklas Luhmann, Ernst von Glasersfeld, Humberto Maturana, Eleanor Rosch, and Francisco Varela, among others, all imagined systems within their constructivist epistemologies. This work hinted at the potency of distributed genius — the concept of an emergent principle of sentience and agency. A pioneering work published by Eugène Marais in 1926, *The Soul of the White Ant*, was an attempt to understand this social phenomenon.

The concept of distributed genius is not mystic new-age thinking; it's a recognition that the observed phenomena of the natural world are present in the realm of the human. We ignore our place within that natural world at our peril. We need to think beyond the limits of exceptionalism that lock us into the trap of our own hubris. We might be able to explain the processes of chemical and electrical communication that coordinate the massive alignment of unicellular creatures in mechanistic terms, consistent with the laws of classical physics. But those methods and terms still can't

Gala Porras-Kim, *Two joined Buddha's hands vessel*, 2017, graphite, Flashe paint on paper, artist's frame, 25.75 x 18.5 x 1.5 inches / Courtesy the artist and Commonwealth and Council. Photo: Ruben Diaz

explain the social effects of affective force in the human cultural world or the social life of other living things.

There are in fact many social systems and phenomena that cannot be explained by the mechanics of direct contact or immediate communicative exchange. The work of biologist Rupert Sheldrake, which focuses on the study of species' transformations and shifts in animal behaviors (called *morphic resonance*) is just one example. But the large-scale rise of corporate fascism, virulent racism, consensual delusion, and other effects of rapid refresh cycles of communication also defy explanation.

The distributed force of emergent agency requires that we come to terms with a concept of genius as an *outcome* as much as a source. If we think of genius as an innate gift, we must think of it as something that works through us — not individually but collectively — in a distributed network. Our illusions of autonomy have long been accompanied by equally grand delusions of individual agency, but these illusions can't contain or deny the forces of distributed genius. The political institutions brought into being within the tenets of these beliefs are also insufficient.

How to reckon with these phenomena? Not by ignoring them, but by coming to terms with the *porousness of identity* and the *aggregation of agency*. We are nodes in a distributed system of co-dependencies, activated by forces that pulse through it. And yet, we are still somehow reassuring ourselves of our capacity to act independently even as the effects of the aggregate erode the foundations of these beliefs. The concept of genius, when inextricably bound to the myth of the autonomous individual, is one of the forces contributing to our collective delusion. Instead, we need to recognize ourselves as elements in a distributed system, living in a condition of within-ness to its holistic operations in mechanistic and non-mechanistic modes. It isn't a matter of definition, it's an essential principle for survival.

IN THE BEGINNING

ISAAC BASHEVIS SINGER

translated from the Yiddish by
David Stromberg

A heat wave spread across Tel Aviv. The "veterans" — the ones who'd live there for a while — called it a *hamsin*. But for the newcomers it was hard to tell the difference between a *hamsin* and just plain heat. A hot, dry wind blew in from somewhere, reminding Liza Fuchs of flames from a furnace. At night, while she slept, her mouth and throat became dry, and her nostrils filled with sandy dust. The sun went down as flaming red as coal, and for a long time after sunset blazing tongues continued to rise as from a heavenly abyss on fire. The moon was unusually large, blood red, a burning globe mapping otherworldly lands. The nights were not still. Voices could be heard in the middle of the night — just like in Warsaw. Young men cried out in Hebrew. Young women laughed. Cars and trucks passed in the streets. There was no war in the country, but neither was there peace. The Polish-language newspaper that Liza bought each morning reported tension on the border. There were skirmishes in the Negev, near Gaza, or whatever those places were called. Against the shine of the moon you could see military trucks and motorcycles driven by soldiers in helmets. A silent mobilization had begun.

At dawn, Liza stood at the window, stark naked. A light wind, smelling of dead fish and sewage, blew in periodically from the sea. Liza's body was both shivering and sweating. Over the flat roofs of Tel Aviv hung little bundles of stars, like fiery bunches of grapes. Cats meowed. A few light poles shone with a yellow light reminding Liza of the lanterns that were carried behind coffins in Warsaw. It was strange to think that she had found herself in the Jewish state, Palestine, Israel. But what good was all this Jewishness to her? She would never learn their Hebrew. She'd tried taking Hebrew classes at an *ulpan*. But right in the beginning, the grammar made her head spin. The Hebrew words, with their *khet*s and their *khaf*s, got stuck in her throat. Perhaps, if she'd come when she was younger, she might have managed to learn a little. But she was over 40. She could just as well forget about understanding anything.

Yes, she might as well say goodbye to everything. She's left without a job, without a husband. She no longer goes to the cafe where the Polish-speaking Jews gather — the Warsaw Manjeks and Salczes who greet each other with *servus* and kiss the women's hands. They leave her sitting alone at her table. The men don't even look at her. The women throw sharp glances at her. The waiters are impolite. They scoop up the few coins she leaves for a tip and don't even say *toda* — thank you. Liza had even tried going to a kibbutz. But she didn't last there more than a week. The sun left a rash on her face. In the dining hall she was eaten by flies. She couldn't stand anything there: the aluminum spoons, the bare tables, the half-naked servers who slammed the plates and bowls, the scent of disinfectant, used to wash down the tile floors. A thick darkness reigned at night, a tropical blackness which no lampposts could illuminate. Snakes slithered in the grass. Bats flew overhead. The frogs quacked with human voices. The crickets didn't chirp — they sawed invisible trees. The jackals howled as in childbirth. Arabs lurked on the other side of the mountain. At the cultural center, the *beit tarbut*, the newspapers and magazines were all in Hebrew. The men at the kibbutz were either too young for her — sabras who knew no language other than Hebrew — or old men who smelled of garlic and groaned when they spoke Yiddish. Here in Tel Aviv, Liza at least had her own apartment, though it didn't have a bathtub or a shower, just a toilet on the roof. She could wash herself at the sink. And even for this rooftop apartment she had to pay 800 lira in key money.

Liza had already done all kinds of work here: cut women's hair, ironed shirts at a cleaner's, even cleaned the rooms of a two-star hotel. But she was now, again, without a job. Her entire fortune consisted of 12 lira and a few coins. She had already stopped making lunch, satisfying herself with bread and *lebenya*, a kind of sour milk that had an aftertaste to which Liza could never quite get accustomed.

Now, after a couple of hours of sleep, Liza stands and looks off into the distance, with her face to the sea, toward Italy, toward Europe. It could have been different. She could have easily gotten a visa to America. She could have now been looking out onto the Broadway lights, which never went out, or at the Hollywood studios. She could have acted in English and been a star. But her bitter luck had carried her here, to the Jewish state, where everything was small, poor, and where you always needed *protektsia* — to know the right people. The civil servants to whom Liza came with all kinds of questions and requests would make her wait, scribble something with their pens, and pretend they couldn't hear her.

What did she actually have in common with these people? It was true, she was Jewish, but she'd never liked Jews. She'd always, since childhood, had an aversion to their black eyes, crooked noses, beards, kaftans, sidelocks. Even worse than the Jews of olden days were the modern Jews — short, fat, with poorly shaven faces, thick forelocks, quick eyes, sly smiles. Their jokes always made her sick. She especially hated the Jewish ladies in their fur coats, who screeched when they spoke Polish, filled all the Polish cafes, pushed themselves into all the Polish *pension* houses, read the newest Polish books. Almost all of Liza's lovers had been Christian. She'd been ready to convert as soon as her mother shut her eyes for good. But the Germans burned her mother in Auschwitz or Treblinka. Liza had been through every kind of hell and had ended

Rodrigo Valenzuela, *Barricade No. 2*, 2017, archival pigment print mounted on Sintra, 55.5 x 45.25 inches (framed)
Courtesy the artist and Klowden Mann Gallery

up in Israel. The years passed like a bad dream. Nothing was left of them but a broken career, a confused mind, a pained heart, and a void that nothing could fill.

Every morning Liza asked herself the same thing: *Why bother getting up? What can this day give me?* But she lacked the courage to commit suicide. The bitter truth was that she lived on daydreams, sexual fantasies. Since leaving her Jewish lover, Edek Grizhendler, the almost-doctor who worked here as an electrician, her only satisfaction has been imagining trips abroad, love affairs, treasures, chance acquaintances. Millionaires fall in love with her and build her theaters. Hollywood magnates see her playing somewhere in a coffeehouse and write up years-long contracts for her. She travels the world in a yacht and everyone loves her to death — from the captain to the last deck-hand. She has a kind of a potion or pill that inflames desires, makes men crazy. A genius playwright shows up, a second Bernard Shaw, who writes plays just for her, Liza Fuchs, and when she acts, the public is constantly amazed. When she sings a song, the audience falls weak. She's crowned Miss Universe, and in every single country a handsome gentleman is chosen to serve her, like a court page.

Liza feels a little cold and goes back to bed. She covers herself with a blanket and lies in silence. Her body is both hot and damp from sweat. The dye that she uses on her hair, which went gray early on, pricks her scalp, and the roots sting. Her whole body feels pinched, stung, and bitten. No, she won't sleep tonight either.

Liza closes the shutters and turns on the light. Her eyelids flicker in the blinding light and she starts looking for something on the shelf. Strange, but despite running away from country after country, and wandering through all kinds of camps, she had nonetheless managed to save an album with photos, flyers, and reviews. She had already decided many times not to go near these yellowing leftovers, but she can't stand the temptation. This is the only proof she has that she once played on the Polish stage, in a small theater, and received some recognition. Her photograph was printed in the Polish press, even in the anti-Semitic newspapers. Liza sits down and again reads what they wrote about her: a promising talent, a rising star, an actress with character, chic, charm. God in heaven! Poland is ruined, the theaters destroyed, the reviewers dead. Nothing was left of the old days except these little scraps of paper, crumbling at the edges. But she can still read the words, look at the pictures and illustrations. Why should the past be any less important than the present? Won't the present pass too? What's left of Mademoiselle Rachel, Sarah Bernhardt, Eleonora Duse? Dust — and binders full of memoirs.

Liza reads and reads. Here and there a critic sticks in a nasty word, and it still stings her breast today, just like that first morning, on the week of the premiere. After a while, Liza puts the album back on the shelf and walks over to the hanging mirror, which has a crack running down the middle. She looks at herself, from all sides like an expert. Her body is still youthful, her bust small, her waist thin, but her hairdo has several shades: blond, brown, yellowish. Her neck has a middle-aged fold, a network of wrinkles. Under her gray eyes hang bluish bags. The only perfect thing is her nose, totally Arian, and the thin lips. *Is it possible that I'm 43 already? Am I the same Liza Fuchs? Can it be that I'm stuck somewhere in Palestine, in Asia, surrounded by wild Arabs, without any hope of ever acting in the theater, or even getting a visa to civilized country?*

It's bad, very bad. Liza turns off the light and goes back to bed. The sheet is damp and full of sand. The pillow too hard. God in heaven! First Hitler tried to make soap out of her, and now she's fallen into a Jewish trap. She'll grow old here, ugly and broken. She'll have nothing left to do but sit on the sidewalk on Ben Yehuda or Allenby Street and beg.

Liza shuts her eyelids and when she opens them again it's daytime. She puts on her robe, lifts the shutters. The sun shines in the pale blue sky, ready to burn for another long day. On the left they're putting up a building. The construction workers are already at work. Down below there are sacks of cement. From the open window frame you can hear the sounds of banging, pounding, cursing. It seems she's gotten up late because the shops are open: the *makolet* or corner store, the *maspera* or hair salon, the *makhleva* or milk shop — even the shop where in the window they have menorahs, candlesticks, spice-holders, and water basins. A tall military man in khakis, with dangling epaulettes on his wrinkled shirt, walks next to a short woman, a soldier with messy hair and sandals on her feet. A man pulls an oil barrel on rubber wheels tied to a little horse. A Yemenite dealer of used clothes calls out with a Yiddish singsong — *alte-zakhen, alte-zakhen* — "old stuff". A blind beggar in a turban, a kaftan that looks like a nightshirt, and two sidelocks as thin as rope, holds out his hand for charity. Liza is astonished anew every single day. *It this really a Jewish state? How did they do it? Who? When? How long can this last?*

A child appears calling out the morning news. Liza listens to his voice. Is it war again? No, at least not for now. But the sun is already beating down on this morning. Her forehead's already completely wet.

2.

The old lady that lived in the apartment across from Liza has suddenly moved away. The doors had always been closed and locked. Now they were spread open, and out of them came a broken piano, chairs, tables, dishes, an icebox. Then painters painted the rooms. When the paint dried, a new neighbor moved in: a little man with a dark face, shiny black eyes, and a white little beard. He yelled at the wagon-carriers in Hebrew and carried his belongings in himself. He had little furniture, but many books. The walls were covered with shelves. The new tenant was dressed in a pair of khaki pants and a blue shirt from which gray chest-hair stuck out. For his age, he was quick and flexible. *Dirty, like all Jews*, thought Liza, *but why does he need such a big library?* Liza kept the door open on account of the heat. He soon stood at the threshold speaking Hebrew to her in a grating voice. She answered him in Polish and he switched to a broken Polish with a Yiddish accent. He threw in Russian words. He told her that he was from somewhere in Lithuania, but that 30 years ago he had spent some time in Warsaw, where he'd been a Hebrew teacher. He asked for a drink of water, and Liza poured him a glass from a bottle that she kept in the icebox. He drank thirstily, like a young man, and drizzled on his little beard. *A Litvak pig*, Liza said to herself, *all the troubles start with them*. He thanked her, put the glass at the edge of the door, and called out, "Has the *pani* lived here long?"

"Too long."

"What's wrong with this place? When I first came, I lived in a *tsrif*, a shed, worse than today's transit camps. The jackals howled all night. I even had malaria. I caught a fever that I still have today."

"So you've become a Zionist?"

"I myself don't know what I've become. Since the gentiles didn't want us, we had to build something of our own."

"The Arabs don't want us either."

"No one asked them!"

He's old, but he talks like a young man, Liza thought. *It seems he has no family.* She watched the man run up and down the stairs, carrying stacks of books, sweating, and wiping his sweat with a dirty handkerchief. His little beard was white, but his eyebrows were black. His pupils looked mean, sharp, full of the kind of ridicule, Liza thought, that only Jews have. She kept looking him over, again and again. He had a kind of Middle Eastern darkness, not unlike the Jews who came from Tunisia, Morocco, or Yemen. It was as if his skin had taken in endless amounts of sun. It seemed to her that a person like him could glow in the dark, like the phosphorescent face of a wristwatch. *Well, what's there to see here?* Liza cut him down in her mind. *A Jew like all the others. A hedgehog on two feet.* She dressed and went out to put an announcement in a German newspaper, where many short-term announcements were made.

God in heaven! She hated everything about this city: the names of the streets, the Hebrew signs, the dark Jews who looked nearly black, the beggars with the wild sidelocks, all the commotion of Tel Aviv. On the bus people pushed and cursed. The conductor was angry. The banknotes with the Hebrew letters were soft and damp like wet rags. At the offices of the German newspaper no one understood her Polish and Liza had to speak Yiddish, a language that disgusted her even more than Hebrew.

She went back home on foot. The heat was beating down on her head, so she sat down next to a table at a sidewalk cafe. A waiter brought her coffee in a metal cup. She took a sip and winced. *They call this coffee, these Jews. It tastes like burnt marsh. I don't have enough strength for this!* decided Liza at once. *It's time to end it.* The thought of suicide always calmed her a little. You could bring the whole thing to an end with some rope or a little bit of poison. If there'd been a gas stove in the apartment, it might have been even easier, but all she had was an oil burner. She paid and continued back home. *Just don't let that Litvak's door be open!* she begged the higher powers. She wanted to lock herself in, be alone. Thank God, the door across from hers was closed. Liza went inside and locked her door. Her clothes were wet and she took them off. She sprawled across the bed and fell asleep — the weary sleep of despair, and of heat that doesn't let up for days, weeks, months …

Liza woke up, drank some water, and was again overtaken by fatigue. *Am I sick or something?* she wondered. She could barely stay on her two feet. *What day is this?* she asked herself. Since coming to Palestine, she'd lost track of the months, days, weeks. Sunday seemed like Monday to her. Winter got mixed up with spring, fall with summer. This place had no seasons. Time stretched into one long heat wave, punctuated only by sudden rains and lazy cold air.

Liza continued to drowse and by the time she woke up it was already evening. Tel Aviv cried out with a summer cry. The air in the room was as warm as a Turkish bath. Though the shutter was closed, large insects had somehow crept in, grasshoppers and moths that flew, buzzed, and bumped into the walls with tropical strength. The boy who brought ice hadn't come today. Just in the worst of heat, they were on strike. The last piece of ice in the icebox melted and everything inside went lukewarm, rotten. In the half-darkness, Liza set down a bowl for the water to drip into. She sat down on a stool, wiped her sweat with a handkerchief, and was suddenly reminded of snow. Had there ever really been such things as snowstorms, frosts, and ice flowers on window panes? Had she really ridden a sled from Zakopane to Morskie Oko, and had her shirt collar really filled up with snowflakes? Had she really spent the night in that cabin at the top of that mountain, and made the acquaintance of Stefan Kruszynski? It all seemed so far away to her, perhaps a hundred years ago. She herself would have considered it all a fantasy were it not for a photograph of her standing on skis, in boots, with thick wool socks and ski poles in her gloved hands. She'd nearly broken her foot then, sliding down the mountain. Stefan Kruszynski caught her in his strong arms and carried her like a special delivery parcel. "Oh, these memories! They'll break what's left of me," said Liza out loud. "Where in the world is Stefan Kruszynski now? He probably fell in the Warsaw Uprising…"

Someone knocked at the door.

"Who's there? One second!"

Liza quickly put on a kimono. She put on her slippers. Perhaps it was an express letter? Perhaps a telegram? But from whom? She opened and saw the neighbor, the Litvak. His little beard had whitened in the evening darkness, lit up by light beams passing through the slats of the shutters.

"What do you want?"

"I hope I haven't disturbed the *pani*. Do you, by any chance, have a little salt?"

An old trick! Liza nearly said. She went looking for the salt shaker on the shelf.

"Here's some salt."

"Thank you very much."

For a moment they stood in the half-darkness, silent and uneasy. Then Liza said,

"Have you maybe heard anything about a job?"

"What kind of job?"

"Whatever. I'm ready to do anything."

"What's the pani's profession?"

"Acting. A Polish actress."

"I see. I don't, unfortunately, know of any jobs, but one can always ask. Why doesn't the pani play in any theater?"

"How? I don't know Hebrew."

"All you have to do is to learn the part."

"I can't even read the Hebrew letters."

"That's easy to learn."

"I've tried. I even went to a — what's it called — an *ulpan*."

"You can, you can. I'm already 63 years old, but if I had to, I'd learn Chinese.

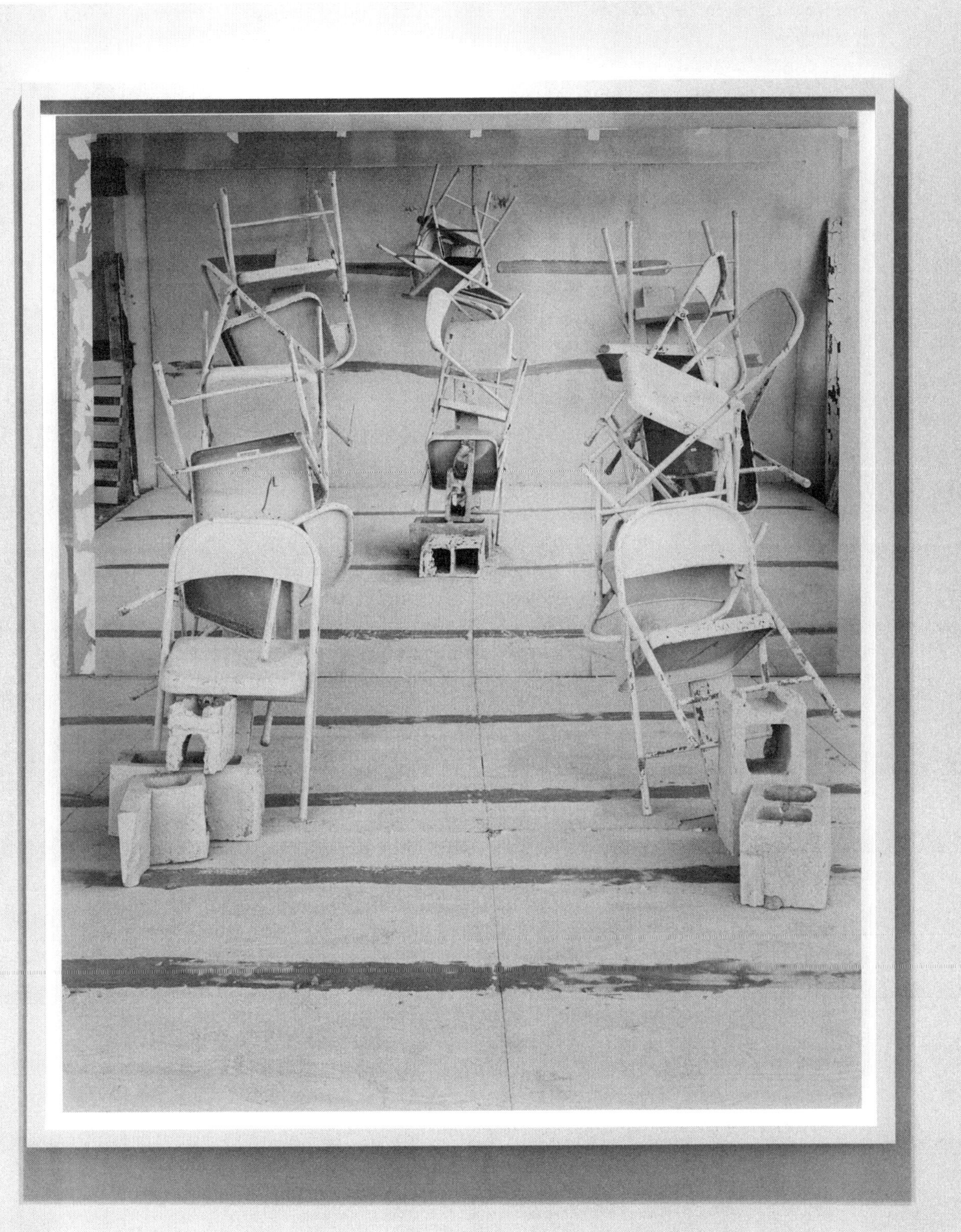

Rodrigo Valenzuela, *Barricade No. 3*, 2017, archival pigment print mounted on Sintra, 55.5 by 45.25 inches (framed) / Courtesy the artist and Klowden Mann Gallery

Before I came to this country, I was a law student, but I've had 30 jobs here, if not more."

"What do you do now?"

"Well, it's a long story. I've argued with all the political parties, and here, without a political party, you're half dead. But I get a pension. A very, very small pension."

"I see."

"If the *pani* would like, I could teach her Hebrew."

"No, I've given up on that. Why would you do that?"

"Oh, just for the sake of it. Because it's sad."

"Well, thank you."

"It's never too late to start over."

"That's what they say in books."

"It's the truth. Look at the Jewish people. After two thousand years they've started up with the same story."

"I'm no Zionist."

"Well, you don't have to be a Zionist. History brought us here by force. Or call it God. If we haven't died, it means we have to live."

"Thanks anyway."

The neighbor left. Liza closed the door after him. For a while it was quiet, as if he'd stayed in the hallway to eavesdrop. Then Liza heard him go back into his apartment. She lay down on the bed again. *Argued with the political parties*, she mumbled. *Obviously also argued with his wife. Those who argue, argue with everyone. Otherwise he wouldn't have that white little beard!* Liza suddenly felt like laughing, crying, yawning, sneezing — all at once. She lay there and listened to her own depths. She'd heard plenty of Zionist propaganda, and it always had the opposite effect on her. But the simple things this Litvak had said returned to her mind again and again: *History had brought us here by force. If we haven't died, it means we have to live.* Yes, the Jews just won't die. How many times had Liza decided to kill herself — and been unable! In this sense, she was a Jew. She couldn't die either. Not by any means.

She got up and washed herself at the sink. *I have to go out into the street! I have to eat something!* The water was cool. Every now and then a grasshopper bumped into her shoulder, neck, stomach, and she peeled it off, flicked it away. *They won't die either, those worms.* Liza washed and soaped herself. Then, in the dark, she put on a dress and a pair of shoes onto her bare feet. She didn't powder her face or put on lipstick. *Yes, I have to eat. Maybe I can still find something …* She opened the door slowly. It seemed the Litvak, too, hadn't completely closed his door, and a line of light shone through. She stretched out her hand and knocked. Footsteps could be heard, as if the neighbor had read her thoughts, and had the whole time listened and waited. He now stood before her and all she could see was that little white beard and two shadowy snares from which his eyes sparkled.

"It's your neighbor," she said. "Do you really want to teach me?"

"I meant what I said."

"When can we start?"

"What about now?"

"Isn't it late?"

"It's not late."

They stood on either side of the threshold, silent, poised, very close, without any apprehension, like people who've wasted many years and have lost all hope. It seemed to Liza that this had already happened. In a dream? On the stage? She thought of her father. She wanted to cry.

"Do you have a workbook?" she asked.

"Yes, I have a workbook."

"I've forgotten it all. Everything that has to do with Jewishness. We have to start in the beginning."

And the neighbor repeated, "Yes, in the beginning…"

MORE LIKE YOU

SLOANE CROSLEY

There are acceptable favorites and unacceptable favorites. Having a favorite flower, for example, is a tacit indication of sophistication and taste, of knowing flowers well enough to pick one. Same thing with a scent, a brand of chocolate, a poet. The broader the category, however, the more juvenile the act of choosing. Favorite colors and animals are the jurisdiction of children, who pick to test their own authority. I'm not quite sure where having a favorite quote falls on this spectrum. But I have one. I fear that a grown woman — nay, a writer — with a favorite quote is not a great look. Still, my loyalty to the following sentiment trumps my embarrassment about picking it:

> *A genius is the one most like himself. — Thelonious Monk*

I think about this quote constantly, almost like a blanky or one of those household products with multiple applications. Like baking soda or tinfoil. It works for when you're feeling jealous or competitive or just idly comparing yourself with others. It faces simultaneously inward and outward. There's a photonegative image within it of a group of people: a room or a dinner party or the whole world. It can be any number you choose, specific or faceless. Then there's the idea that the quote was not originally meant for me, but for jazz musicians. This takes the fangs out of it, stops it from staring me directly in the eye like this classic, whose attribution to Hemingway is much debated:

> *There is nothing to writing. All you do is sit down at a typewriter and bleed.*

The Monk quote on the other hand, strikes at the heart of what it is to be a genius. It humanizes genius but not at the expense of true intellect. You may be sitting across from a Fields Medal–winning, Pulitzer Prize–sporting Prix Goncourt finalist, but

Monk's measure of genius is less about titles than it is about efficiency. How much of your brain's potential has made it outside of your brain? It's a valve issue, not a reservoir issue. On the surface, it's too accepting of an idea. There are a lot of stupid and ineffectual people in this world who are the most like themselves. One of them is our president. If we take Monk literally, our commander in chief is a genius. But if we assume he's already referring to a group of curious people with talent and heart, then this quote becomes the perfect by-a-nose criterion. It's useful socially as well, a means of separating the blowhards from the sages.

Every mental endeavor in the world, be it art or mathematics or science, exists to get closer to the truth. The closer you get to the truth of yourself, the closer you get to the truth of everyone else. You become the one most like yourself so that you can come out the other side.

excerpts from

THE KINGDOM OF SURFACES

SALLY WEN MAO

Looking-glass House

On a spring afternoon, I emerge from the 77th Street Lexington station, on my way to a newly opened exhibition at the Met called *China: Through the Looking Glass.* Andrew Bolton, the curator, names his introduction of the exhibition "Toward an Aesthetic of Surfaces." Alluding to Barthes, Voltaire, Swift, it's a love letter to artifice. A love letter to pastiche.

Are the surfaces of these fantasies fragile, are they strong enough to break my fingers? Inside the exhibition, I peer at the displays. The glass vitrines hold cinnabar screens, porcelain, cloisonné enamel bowls from lustrous dynasties. Silks and sequins, sumptuous textures — otherworldly like fish scales stolen from the bodies of real creatures. I am searching for the Looking Glass house, a portal. The surface doesn't dissolve magically to the touch. This surface is a mirror, a seam. To love a pretty object because it is not allowed to be touched. To love a pretty object as time colludes with its disappearance. To disappear into enchantment.

Do these surfaces awe me? My own yes disturbs me.

The Garden of Live Flowers

In Lewis Carroll's tome, glass is not a border — in fact, it becomes immaterial, a silvery mist you can breathe in. Opacity has a way of tricking us into believing something is impenetrable. Glass becomes gauze becomes haze, and in that haze, the little girl enters the mirror.

Entering the mirror, I forget who I am. I forget what I'm wearing — a blue cornflower dress with an empire waist, stitched in a silk factory by the hands of a young woman in China. The early Buddhist sculpture hall displays what the curators call a Bamboo Garden. Here is a fiber-optic kingdom — a thousand plexiglass rods emit LED lights. Their silvery forms move like anemones. The bamboo LED forest snakes around the Buddhist sculptures, trapping the mannequins inside. The mannequins wear pretty hats designed by a milliner from London.

They face a window to a garden of infernal flora. The flowers of perdition, all red. Opium poppies, the landscape I can't quite make out. I touch the lattice frame and a hole opens on its surface. The world tears violently open like silk.

There are no wild silkworms left in the world. For humans to harvest silk, the silkworm has to die. Cocoons thrown in boiling water. If the silkworm survives and becomes a silk moth, the silk is ruined. Everything beautiful at its kernel suggests suffering, death.

Wool and Water

I am trapped in someone else's imagination. My borders lose shape. I become a woman without boundaries, permeable as water. From my mouth, sepals fall. From my skin, armor and scales slough off. I am a silkworm before the harvest. In my throat, a protest — but no sound escapes, except the soporific sound of a reed flute.

In the next hall, there is a party. Is this…the Met Gala? The flowers of perdition lavish the museum, a paradise. Women dressed like empresses get in formation. Rihanna in gold Guo Pei and fox furs, Beyoncé in a Givenchy gown, Fan Bingbing in a peacock green cape — all of these costumes I've seen only on the internet. At the end of their procession, the Red Queen walks. She wears a red wool shawl over her gown made of pink opium poppies, and her crown is wrapped around her neck. An aquiline mask shrouds her face. She takes it off, revealing herself as Anna Wintour. "You!" she shouts, pointing at me. "You are not on the guest list."

Humpty Dumpty

Lewis Carroll published *Through the Looking-Glass, and What Alice Found There* in 1871, the same year as the Chinese Massacre in Los Angeles, where 17 Chinese immigrants were robbed, tortured, and hanged by a mob of more than 500 white men in a single alley in what is now downtown, near Union Station. It was the largest mass lynching in American history.

The 1870s, the height of the Gilded Age, when moguls built monuments out of blood sacrifices. 1871, one decade after the Second Opium War. 1871, two years after the completion of the Transcontinental Railroad. 1871, one decade before the Chinese Exclusion Acts. 1871, 16 years before the Snake River Massacre, which left the bodies of 31 Chinese men dead in a dusky Oregon valley called Hell's Canyon. In one ranch home, a Chinese skull was fashioned into a decorative sugar bowl.

If you decontextualize the history from the bowl and place it on a kitchen table, what do you have? A varnished object whose function is to hold sugar. Sugar sweetened the ranch hand's morning coffee, sweetened the whipping cream, the cakes and tarts. The purpose of sugar — pleasure. Sensation. What a treat. Skull, sockets, 19th-century cane field. If you place the decorative sugar bowl in a museum exhibition, what does it become?

THE RISE AND FALL OF THE FILOSOFESSA

MASSIMO MAZZOTTI

The myth of the child prodigy is familiar to all of us. A boy, tutored by his father, captures the public imagination. He achieves remarkable things by adolescence; his genius is performed for public spectacle; his life and work become part of public record. The young man makes history. And often, of course, the recognized genius is a young man.

And yet, for a brief period in European history, the story went a little differently. During the first half of the 18th century, in certain parts of Europe — northern Italy in particular — the most celebrated child prodigies were girls. This phenomenon flourished in otherwise inhospitable circumstances: girls and women didn't have access to formal education at the time and little legal or social standing. They were not, by any means, treated the same as boys were. And yet, some of these girl geniuses went on to become distinguished and learned women in modern sciences — most notably in mathematics, physics, and medicine.

One of the most acclaimed female child prodigies was Maria Gaetana Agnesi (1718–1799), whose 300th birthday we celebrate this year. Agnesi eventually grew into a learned woman, or *filosofessa*, and, in 1748, became the first woman to publish a mathematics book. Two years later, she became the first woman invited to lecture on mathematics at a university. The offer came from Bologna, one of the largest and most prestigious universities in Europe at the time. (Remarkably, Bologna already had a woman on its faculty: Laura Bassi, professor of experimental physics, and, yes, another former child prodigy. Agnesi was also nominated to the Academy of Sciences in Bologna, which had a startling number — at least five — Italian and French women among its members during that period.) Her book, hailed by the Parisian Academy of Sciences as an excellent systematization of the new techniques of integral and differential calculus, was translated into French and English, and used as a textbook for decades.

Agnesi seems to have been part of a phenomenon that historians have long struggled to make sense of. Why was so much attention dedicated to identifying and nurturing female academic talent in northern Italy? Why on earth did Agnesi decide to study advanced mathematics? And how did a woman come to be perceived as a credible mathematician? More specifically, how did Agnesi find her way through a rigidly gendered scientific environment, and establish herself as a legitimate scholar?

This remarkable story is, of course, not the beginning of progressive female inclusion. The height of her scientific career, from the 1720s to the early 1750s, coincided with the peak of the phenomenon around female child prodigies and scholars. By her death in 1799, that world was long gone and Agnesi's name was nearly erased from the annals of science — along with the names of the other accomplished and learned women of this period. What had happened? Was there a connection between the brief acknowledgment of young, genius girls and their eventual demise?

To answer these questions we need to listen to Agnesi's long-lost voice. This means steering clear of facile dichotomies and suspiciously linear narratives. Instead, we need to focus on Agnesi's own experience, and how she made sense of the world she inhabited.

ENTERING THE *CONVERSAZIONE*

Agnesi was born in 1718 to a wealthy Milanese family, which had built its fortune in the luxury textile trade. By the age of five, she was already entertaining friends and visitors by speaking foreign languages and reciting poetry. At nine, she gave a famous and documented oration defending the right of women to access all kinds of knowledge, including the sciences. The monologue, which was probably a Latin translation exercise written by her tutor, stunned the audience gathered at her family's palazzo. It was in fact, so impressive that it was published in 1729, in a collection of essays on the question of women's education. The child had tapped into a broader issue circulating at the time. There were new and modern ideas about liberty and justice, and perhaps the time had come to question women's subordinate status. Earlier versions of the *querelle des femmes* had mostly taken the form of male-dominated exercises in erudition, but the question had assumed a more urgent tone in those years. In more pedagogical terms — the terms that concerned Agnesi — the central question was: Should women be allowed to study whatever they wished?

Agnesi, at least, certainly did just that. By the 1730s, she had grown into a learned and combative adolescent, but unlike her brothers, she could not seek admission to boarding school. Her father Pietro, however, was determined to give his daughter an extensive and advanced education, hiring the best tutors in the humanities and sciences. Newtonianism was just then spreading across the continent, and Agnesi was soon privy to its concepts and ideas. She completed her studies at the age of 20, and published her theses, just as any successful university student might have done at the time. Her theses displayed an impressive breadth of philosophical and scientific knowledge, revealing some of the distinctive inclinations that would later guide Agnesi's career: her defense of Newtonian doctrines against continental opponents, and her passion for mathematics. Mathematics, she wrote, "makes us reach and contemplate truth, of which nothing is more delightful."

By that point, Agnesi had become a fascinating and slightly unsettling public attraction. Visitors from all corners of Europe gathered for nightly events at her palazzo in Milan, craving to see the famed *filosofessa* with their own eyes. According to a variety of sources, the audience would gather around in a circle — up to 30 or 40 people at a time — in a richly decorated salon to listen to her debate controversial topics in natural philosophy and mathematics. Typically, these debates would take the form of an academic disputation. Agnesi would confront authoritative opponents — university professors, high-ranking ecclesiastics, and prominent visitors — on topics like the origin of spring waters, or the nature of light and colors. These were well-structured theatrical performances framed by music and refreshments. This kind of gathering was called a *conversazione* — literally, a conversation.

Some of these evenings were well documented. Two French gentlemen recounted their trip to the Agnesi *conversazione* in their letters home. They visited on a hot summer evening in 1739; upon entering, they were unexpectedly invited to engage in a conversation with Agnesi on a scientific topic of their choice. Since the room was filled with people "from all the nations of Europe," they were asked to conduct the discussion in Latin, so that everyone could understand. One of the Frenchmen was puzzled by this unusual request but agreed. He described putting his glass of iced water down to address the lady in rusty Latin. For about an hour, they discussed theories of body-soul relations, a primary scientific concern at the time. His friend, who asked permission to speak in French, stepped in after, changing the subject to the properties of certain geometrical curves. For her part, Agnesi continued to speak in Latin, and those who could not follow her reasoning were nonetheless able to enjoy her Ciceronian eloquence. "She spoke like an angel," one of the Frenchmen commented.

When the discussion ended, Agnesi's younger sister, Maria Teresa, herself a musical child prodigy, played the harpsichord and sang. As the long summer evening turned into night, candles were lit, sorbets were served, and everyone rose from their chairs to join the general conversation. Agnesi now played the gracious host, greeting the guests, addressing them in French, German, Spanish, or Greek. She returned to talk to the two Frenchmen, saying that she was sorry that their first meeting had taken that peculiar form. She also expressed ambivalence about these kinds of public discussions: for the two people who are truly excited, she quipped, 20 are bored to death. The Frenchmen, who had entered the palazzo with some skepticism, left in awe.

What made Agnesi such an intriguing public figure was her resistance to familiar types of womanhood. Her striking skills — profound learning, social acumen, scholarly bravery, debating ability — were coupled with a fervent religiosity and what might at the time have been called virtuous modesty. Agnesi did not fit the model of the French *salonnière*, but was equally far removed from the ideal of silent femininity promoted by the Counter-Reformation. She had not been trained to keep silent. In fact, she had mastered rhetorical techniques and, in the opinion of witnesses, her ease of speech far surpassed that of boys her age, even those who had been schooled in the best Jesuit colleges. Her disputational skills belonged to the masculine spaces of the boarding school and the university, where students would routinely compete against opponents (often the teachers themselves) learning how to defend or attack a thesis. Seeing a young woman publically perform this dialectical art proved fascinating and perturbing: no wonder she became a veritable magnet for literati, aristocrats, magistrates, politicians, and powerful dignitaries of the Holy Roman Empire.

Agnesi's Choices

Agnesi's glittering life was not without its costs. Intense study and continual performances probably contributed to a mysterious "malady" in her teenage years. The worst of it seemed to strike when Agnesi was 14, after she lost her mother and her favorite tutor. This was undoubtedly too much loss even for such a brave and determined adolescent. Her father hired physicians who specialized in "convulsions," and though they tried various regimes of physical exercise, it was to little avail. A friend reported that on one occasion, Agnesi attempted to jump off a balcony in one of the family's country villas, but she was stopped just in time. This difficult period in Agnesi's life was coupled with an unusual documentary blackout. It isn't clear how Agnesi recovered but it was later credited to the direct intercession of Saint Cajetan, her patron saint. The malady seemed to last about a year, after which, Agnesi dutifully returned to her studies and public engagements.

This return wasn't surprising. Pietro Agnesi was zealous in supporting his daughter's education and scientific work. While we have no direct evidence of his motives, the family's finances are revealing. Pietro was the first in his family to distance himself from trade and warehouses, making an obvious effort to buy his entrance into the Milanese patriciate. In order to live like nobility, the household overspent — constantly. Pietro also made investments specifically designed to elevate the family's social status, rather than yield any significant income. He purchased, for example, unproductive land that came with a feudal title. His daughter's extraordinary talent was a key element in this

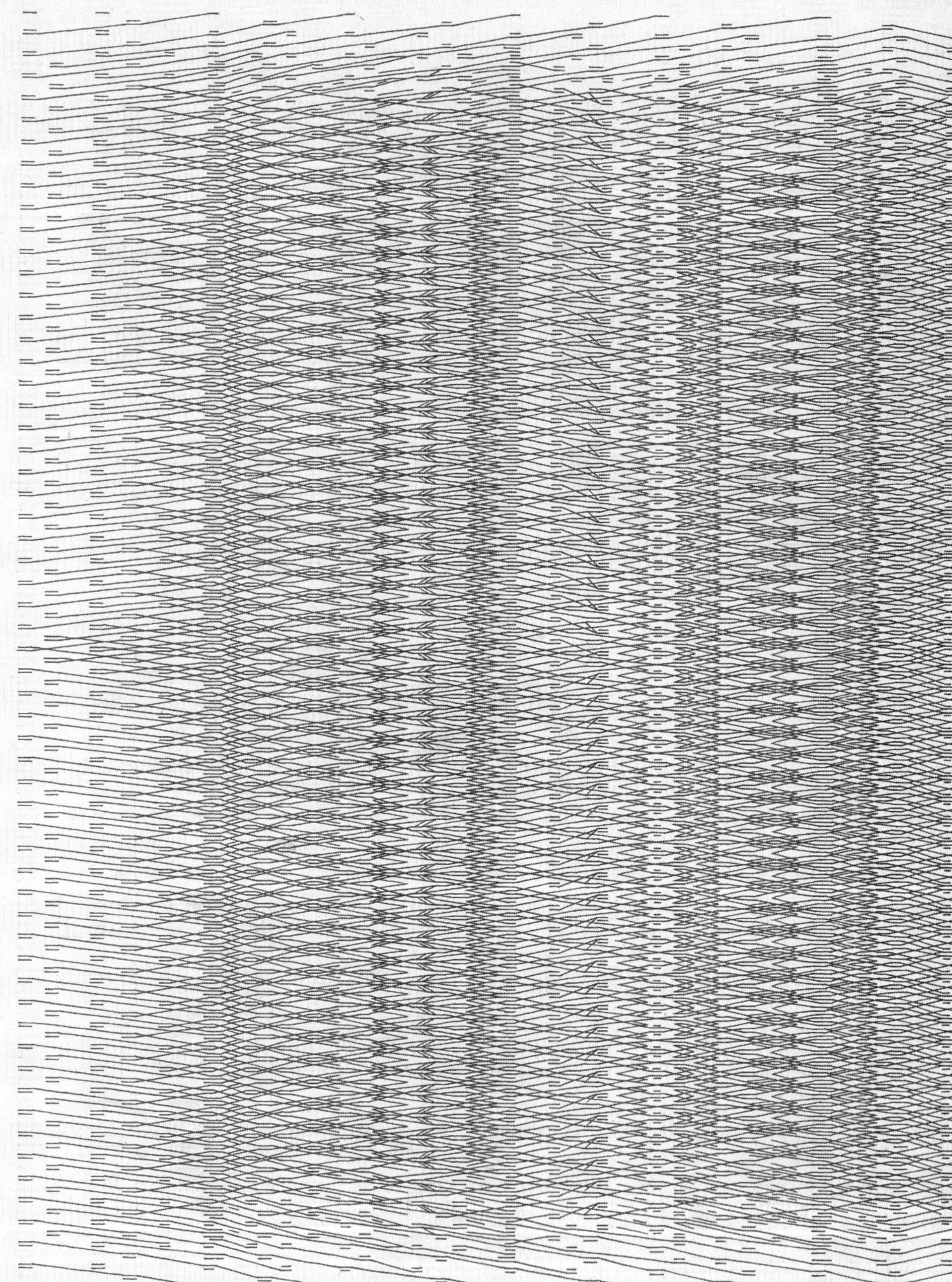

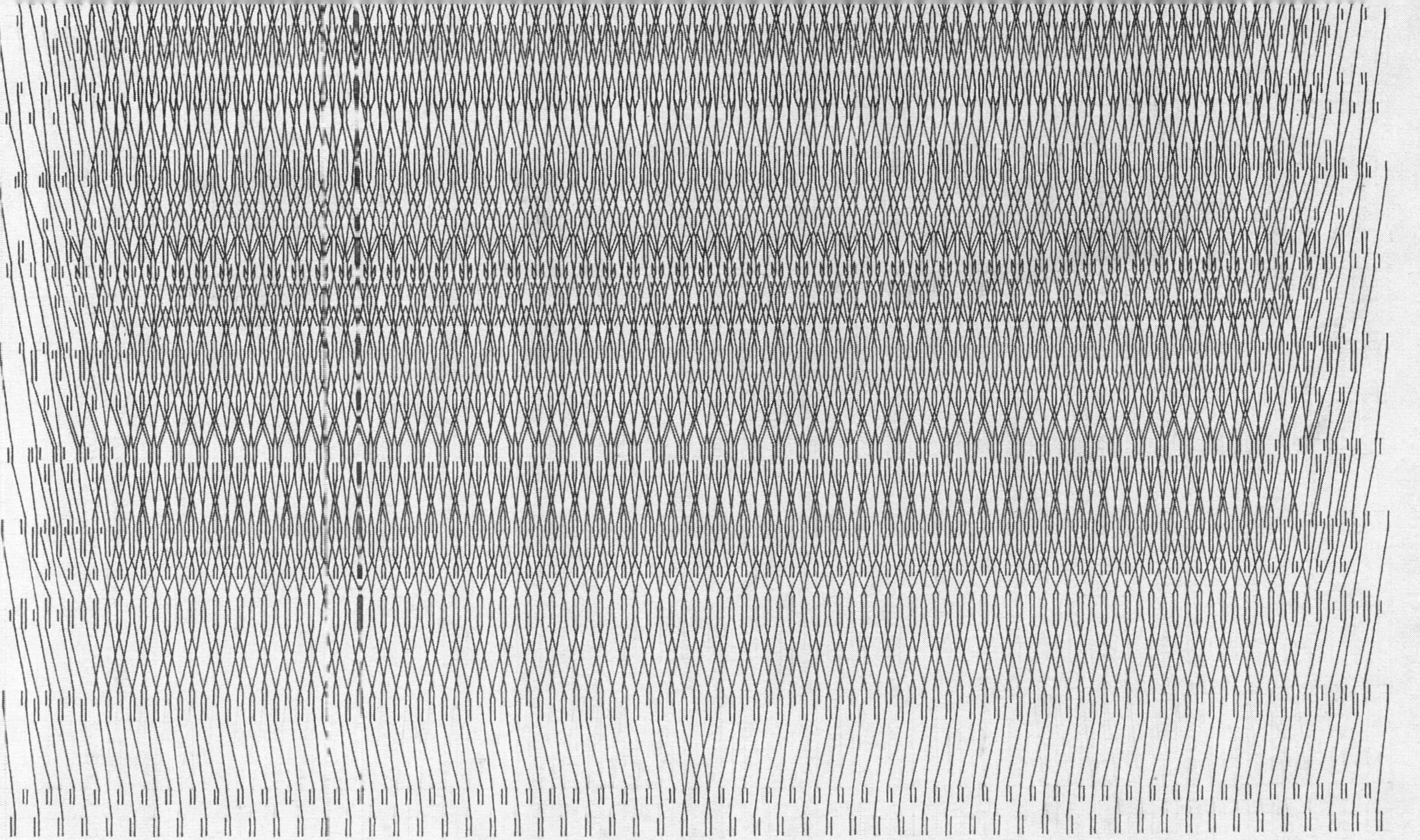

Brian Randolph, *Plenum*, 2018, pen and pencil on paper, 22 x 15 1/2 inches

ment in this strategy, because it attracted the attention of Milanese and imperial elites. Pietro helped her assemble an impressive library, purchase scientific instruments, and work with first-rate mentors. In return, he expected her to engage in domestic performances at his behest. She, however, grew impatient with the life he decreed.

On one occasion, when Agnesi was studying in a quiet country villa, he called her back to Milan to perform for the heir to the throne of Poland. She was not on the original program for this visit, but the prince wanted to meet the *filosofessa*. Grudgingly, the 20-year-old Agnesi got in the gilded carriage sent for her, and duly performed two scientific disputations as effectively and brilliantly as ever. A few days later, writing to a former tutor, she ironically commented on how "appropriately" she and her sister had behaved, and how the prince, like other powerful men before him, had only come to "fill his eyes with pleasurable visions". She was already thinking about withdrawing from her public life.

Eventually, Agnesi told her father that she would become a nun if their routine didn't change. She wanted to dress down, to detach herself from his obsession with luxury. She also wanted to be exempt from going to the theater, parties, and the other rituals of the Milanese elite. She offered to join her father's *conversazione*, but more sparingly, at her will and not his. She wanted to concentrate on studying what really mattered to her: mathematics and theology. She also wanted to live in the real world — "in the century," as she put it. These were difficult years in Milan — years of war and stagnation — and Agnesi could see the moral and physical destitution right outside her palazzo. She was appalled by the living conditions of the poor women and children she saw on the street. She was determined to take part in the world, and to help the people who needed her. A family friend recalled that for a while it looked as if Pietro had been struck by lightning. But it was thanks to Agnesi, that his *conversazione* had reached international visibility: he had no choice but to accept her demands.

Intellectual Pleasures and Earthly Saintliness

By the mid-1740s, Agnesi was one of few Italian specialists who had mastered the techniques of differential and integral calculus. At that time, calculus was the newest and most promising branch of mathematics. The discipline was undergoing rapid expansion mainly because it could so powerfully represent varied empirical phenomena. Calculus was especially effective at modeling processes of physical change, such as the trajectory of a cannon ball, or the water flow of a river.

Jacopo Riccati, one of the pioneers of calculus, lived in the Republic of Venice, whose very existence depended on the management of watercourses. Agnesi reached Riccati through one of her tutors, and they began a rich correspondence. She was determined to refine her understanding of key concepts and techniques and so she plied him with-questions. He later confessed to a friend that it wasn't long before she was taking his suggestions in directions he could not have imagined. She was doing her own thing.

Up to that point, research on calculus had appeared in various periodicals and pamphlets published across Europe. According to Agnesi, these disparate publications yielded methodological inconsistencies and made it difficult for newcomers to find their way through the literature, and so she started planning a book that would offer a coherent systematization of the new field. In order to ensure consistency and methodological cohesion, Agnesi oversaw all aspects of the publication. The publisher's printing press was moved to her palazzo, so that she could supervise the typesetters, who had never worked with calculus symbols before. The two elegant volumes of *Analytical Institutions,* were published in 1748. Agnesi's book was the first well-structured and accessible presentation of this burgeoning mathematical field. The book was not only celebrated at the time — the French Academy of Sciences for example, praised its clarity and innovative methodology — it also became a standard reference text for future generations. Decades later, famed mathematician Joseph-Louis Lagrange still recommended its second volume as the best available introduction to calculus.

Agnesi's work stood out within the existent literature, in part because rival texts were typically just collections of examples and problem-solving techniques. These were toolboxes for practitioners who wanted to use calculus to tackle empirical problems. Agnesi's systematic approach, on the other hand, was based on an entirely different perspective. As she explained in a letter to Riccati, she was interested in the parts of calculus that were not dependent on empirical states of affairs. The study of many curves, she wrote, "I left aside on purpose," as she did not want to get bogged down "with physical matters," but rather wanted to focus on "pure analysis." In other words, Agnesi was not interested in calculus because of its modeling power. Instead, she aimed to teach the reader a way of reasoning, characterized by extreme intellectual rigor. Ultimately, calculus was, for her, an extension of Euclidean geometry — it should therefore achieve the same level of precision and certainty. In fact, because it dealt with abstract concepts like infinity, calculus required a superior intellectual effort; for her, this was the most sublime of intellectual exercises, and, as such, the source of unparalleled delight.

By thinking about calculus in this way, Agnesi revitalized older Platonic and Cartesian traditions, as well as the views of her favorite natural philosopher, Isaac Newton. But she did this using the new form of continental calculus. Her book was therefore distinctive — it focused on the new mathematics itself rather than its applications.

Despite its influence, 19th- and 20th-century historians of science paid little attention to Agnesi's book. The few who leafed through its pages dismissed its unusual features as signs of Agnesi's inadequacy: "While learning calculus," wrote a historian in the 1980s, "she does not wish to study rational mechanics as well!" Riccati knew better: Agnesi was making deliberate choices, which ran against the grain of contemporary scientific practice. The form of the book owed much to its pedagogical purpose, but it also catered to a particular vision of mathematics and its intellectual and spiritual relevance.

Indeed, for Agnesi, mathematics could also make a difference in spiritual life. She was steeped in a philosophical tradition that regarded the "capacity of attention" as a desirable spiritual quality, and calculus, in this view, could be seen as a powerful training tool. She could use it to improve her concentration and in so doing, turn its practice into a form of "natural prayer." Agnesi's religiosity, grounded in meditation and intellectual exercise, was in fact at odds with the prevailing baroque sensibility. This "reasonable" religiosity, as it was sometimes called, was built on the capacity to direct attention to mathematical analyses every bit as much as the signs of the passion of Christ. In one manuscript fragment, for example, Agnesi described feeling her soul "rise" through such meditation. For her, this notion of "attention" thus brought scientific and religious life together in a profound and counterintuitive way.

Charity was another pillar of her religiosity. She taught poor girls and organized a network of parish schools. She financially supported women who were heads of households, and offered assistance to ailing women who could not take care of themselves. At one point, she turned a wing of her family palazzo into an infirmary. Absorbed as she was by her new projects, Agnesi never did go to Bologna to take up her position, although her name figured in the university's books for many years. In fact, she gradually abandoned scientific life. To close friends, she explained that she had written her book of mathematics because she hoped it would be useful to scholars and students. Now, however, she had other plans in mind.

During the last three decades of her life, Agnesi directed the female section of a large charitable institution assisting the urban poor and infirm. She faced the new task with her usual determination, pushing out protégés of the Austrian governor, who had turned it into a lucrative business. She knew perfectly well that she was stepping on toes. Her directorship, she wrote in a letter, was causing "great disgust" among the institute's administrators, as "it takes away from them part of that absolute power that they desire so strongly." Through her work, Agnesi became a role model for many "enlightened Catholics" who combined Catholic tradition with the methods and results of the new science. Her social work was exemplary of a new kind of lay charity in the service of "public happiness," designed to replace baroque models of otherworldly saintliness.

The Mind Has No Sex

Agnesi dedicated *Analytical Institutions* to the most powerful woman in Europe at the time: Maria Theresa of Austria, who had successfully defended her right to rule after seven years of war. Agnesi presented it as a collection "of the luminous progresses of human intellect," and argued that if ever there was a time for women to follow the rapid flights of science, it was then, "when a woman rules with universal admiration." "All women," Agnesi continued, should join the empress and "work for the glory of their sex."

After the publication of *Analytical Institutions*, Agnesi received many letters of congratulations from across Europe, but one in particular stood out. It was a personal note from the pontiff, Benedict XIV, who exhibited some knowledge of the book's contents and mentioned his own studies of analysis as a young man. He wrote again two years later, to announce that he had recommended appointing Agnesi as a lecturer in mathematics at the University of Bologna, then under pontifical rule. The academic senate approved the appointment in 1750. The pontiff thus granted Bologna, his home city, the honor of having two famous learned women — Bassi and Agnesi — on its faculty.

Benedict was sympathetic to Agnesi's enlightened Catholicism. In fact, he hoped that more Catholic scholars would engage with the new science, thereby returning Catholicism to the forefront of Western culture. He also endorsed the enlightened Catholics' fight against all forms of baroque and superstitious religiosity, favoring "reasonable devotion," which valued the believer's intellect, education, and social utility. Most importantly, he was keen to have more women take up leading roles in religious life at a time when traditional elites were growing detached from its collective rites. In a related move, Benedict also modified canon law so that women could produce evidence during processes of canonization, thus giving them unprecedented social and epistemological legitimacy. This kind of Catholicism was so much on the rise that paintings and depictions of the "Education of the Virgin" enjoyed a certain currency in Catholic Europe at the time.

This is not to say that enlightened Catholics argued for the right of women to have generalized access to higher education — quite the contrary: they mostly argued against it. But they also avoided the claim that women were intellectually unfit for science. Most authors subscribed to a rigidly dualistic Christian anthropology, according to which the mind belongs to the spiritual component of the human being, and not to the material body. (Some late 17th century Cartesians had already argued for women's cognitive equality on the basis of a similar dualism; they adhered to the principle that "the mind has no sex.")

This egalitarianism existed only in principle however; it was continuously undermined by the practice of excluding women on social and moral grounds. A popular enlightened Catholic book on women's education published in 1740 concluded that the only women who could safely devote themselves to the study of science and mathematics were "childless widows and wealthy virgins." The learned woman was thus not an oxymoron but an exception.

A significant number of women were, however, able to join the debate. Using Agnesi as an example, Gaetana Secchi Ronchi, a poet from the provincial town of Guastalla, declared that women, surely, had not been vouchsafed "spirit and virtue" to support the tyranny of men. The Tuscan Aretafila Savini de' Rossi, who saw herself as a defender of the new science and its empirical methods, asked that all women, noble and commoner, be able to access formal education. At the center of one of her essays was the assumption that "God created all of our souls equal, giving them the same powers, and these veils that cover our souls are not biased in their substance." Therefore, "one cannot justly deny women that assistance that contributes to self-knowledge and a sense of one's own dignity." The universal access to a formal education, she argued, would not produce social disruption but, on the contrary, it would be beneficial to both family life and the public good.

Closer to Agnesi, in Milan, other women were making their presence felt in the literary world. In 1719, the noblewoman Clelia Borromeo del Grillo — who, a visitor reported, "[spoke] Arabic like the Koran" and was passionate about physics and mathematics — founded a scientific academy in her own palazzo, enlisting prominent natural philosophers and mathematicians from across Italy. Commoners, like Francesca Manzoni, also rose to scholarly fame. Manzoni too was a child prodigy, who in her 20s became an authority in the study of Latin patristic literature. She was also granted imperial patronage for her work as a poet. Many of her compositions celebrated local women like Agnesi who "make our sex proud," and whose capacities "silence those who hate the learned woman."

Battle for the Female Mind

These advocates of women's cognitive equality faced a growing misogynist reaction. Around 1750, at the height of his daughter's fame, Pietro Agnesi was openly criticized for keeping her and her sister in social limbo for his own purposes, precluding them from marriage or the convent. Pietro actually quarreled with the governor of Milan on this particular issue. After the clamorous argument, Pietro suffered a "violent chest pain" and died.

Meanwhile, the haughty, learned woman was becoming a recognizable character in innumerable plays and novels. In these stories, women's learning went hand in hand with arrogance and moral corruption, to the point that the term *filosofessa* assumed a derogatory meaning. Powerful and dissolute ladies were described as keeping books of Locke and Newton in their boudoirs, where they discussed scientific matters in depraved "modern conversations." The men who participated in such conversations were represented as not only effeminate but complicit in an aberrant inversion of the power relationship between the sexes.

The *conversazione*, an important site of female acculturation, was thus ridiculed and morally condemned, while the private tutors hired to teach women were portrayed as abdicating their natural rights in favor of "stupid subjugation." Cities like Bologna and Milan, where learned women had been an especially visible and active presence, attracted the contempt of myriad observers who marveled at female "despotic power," and dominion over "husbands and ministers." In Milan, a French envoy reported disapprovingly, women enjoyed "great credit," to the point that their "bizarre will" was more respected than the "lights of Reason."

This reference to "Reason" was not a coincidence. Savini de'Rossi, like other educated women, was convinced that modern science was on her side in the battle for cognitive equality, but it was actually moving in the opposite direction. Gradually, new "evidence", which was deemed "highly scientific" at the time, transformed the debate: the female mind was dismissed as unsuited to rational thought. Agnesi called these attempts to naturalize women's cognitive inferiority a "philosophical aberration" but they gained a strong foothold in the culture.

One of the texts that contributed to this "aberration" was a widely-circulated letter written by Antonio Conti. The letter, published in 1756, addressed the question of women's intellectual fitness for scientific and political life in self-consciously enlightened and studiously impartial terms. Conti had a materialistic theory of the mind. He believed that human thought resulted from the vibration of brain fibers, much like sound results from the vibration of a string. An ample vibration corresponded with a clear idea, a feeble vibration with a confused one. Referencing contemporary literature on anatomical difference, Conti argued that female bodies were necessarily less vigorous than the bodies of men, simply unfit for rigorous thought. Aside from the fact that they were essentially reproductive in function, this was proven by the lesser consistency and elasticity of the fibers constituting female organs. According to Conti, a woman's body was also awash in fluids — the fibers were submerged in liquid — and so it was altogether lacking in solidity and elasticity. Conti also ventured that the fibers of a female brain were softer than a man's — a softer brain made for a weaker mind.

Interestingly enough, like Agnesi, Conti placed the capacity for attention at the center of intellectual activity. He understood that capacity however, in very different terms: attention was a function of the number and duration of the cerebral fibers' vibrations. For him, attention is what allowed the mind to generate abstract and complex ideas, and so it logically followed that the female mind was severely limited in all disciplines, but especially in logic and mathematics.

Conti's was just one of many physiological arguments against female education articulated across Europe at the time. With the enlightened Catholics, a learned woman was an exception. According to these new scientists, however, she simply couldn't exist.

The Thinking Uterus

By the 1770s, physiological arguments for the intellectual inferiority of women had become mainstream science. Misogyny was scientized, especially, as one might guess, in places where women played a significant role in scientific life. In Bologna, for instance, Petronio Zecchini published a booklet in 1771 on how women think. Zecchini, an anatomist and a young professor of medicine, worked in the shadow of famed anatomist Anna Morandi. He tried to make his mark by distancing himself from those "brutal philosophers" who, like Conti, argued that matter can think. But he could not, he said, exclude the possibility that the body might act on the mind, and affect its cognitive abilities. Indeed, the idea that the female body influenced female thought and behavior was a widely held opinion. Based on anatomical evidence, Zecchini asserted with great confidence that the highly innervated organ responsible for women's "singular way of reasoning" was the uterus.

The uterus "makes women think," he argued, thus accounting for their extravagant habits, lustful desires, emotional instability, faulty logic, and, most importantly, for their congenital incapacity for focusing their attention. Women were therefore incapable of sound and systematic reasoning. This brought him to a conclusion about Agnesi herself: she couldn't possibly be the author of the book published under her name, she must have taken credit for the work of a tutor.

The "thinking uterus," a term coined by Zecchini himself, captured the imagination of Bolognese physicians, literati, and high society at the time. Even the aging Giacomo Casanova, who was living in Bologna at the time, paid attention. Casanova, whose seductions increasingly required financial support, quickly penned a satirical pamphlet poking fun at Zecchini and arguing for the effect that sperm had on a man's mind. On a more serious note however, Casanova also argued that minds were shaped by education and social condition rather than physical states. Allegedly innate female traits, like vanity for example, were "artificial virtues" that responded to expectations, rather than the effect of a woman's body on her mind. The pamphlet was popular — and earned Casanova a pretty penny — but his resistance to the Enlightenment was increasingly in the minority. The impulse to naturalize the links between sex, mind, and social role was beginning to win out.

In 1793 a conservative Catholic author published a satire about a woman who tried to become a natural philosopher. The book was dedicated to Agnesi, who had at least been "wise enough" to renounce her scientific career. By that point in the century, this kind of attitude was standard. Women's physical and intellectual inadequacy was taken for granted. The contemporary literature on education followed suit, stressing women's inadequate capacity for abstract thought and apparently limitless sentimentality. Women were recast as "the moral sex."

Clearly, the sun had set on the world of the *filosofesse*.

Epilogue

Even though the career patterns of these learned women vary, we can nonetheless identify certain broader conditions that made it possible for them to be perceived as credible scholars. These include the relatively benevolent views of so-called enlightened Catholics, who were sympathetic to women's education and involvement in public life. They also refused to differentiate between male and female minds based on physiological considerations. This is what we might call an exceptionality model: women are generally fit for the study of science, and some might even excel at it, but their access should be severely restricted on social and moral grounds. In most cases, this exceptionality was actually fashioned and controlled through the phenomenon of the child prodigy. The uneven geographical distribution of learned women seems consistent with this idea, as does the rapid decline of their status and credibility, which followed the demise of enlightened Catholicism, and the radicalization of the political and cultural debate in the 1760s.

Agnesi died of pneumonia in 1799. Milan was under French military occupation, and religious processions were temporarily forbidden. She was buried quickly, at night, in a common grave; later attempts to identify her remains were unsuccessful. The circumstances of her physical disappearance are emblematic of the process of erasure that was already under way at the time of her death. She essentially had to be rediscovered, around 1900, by the author of her first modern biography, the early Italian feminist Luisa Anzoletti.

A serious assessment of Agnesi's scientific achievements, however, would have to wait even longer. The naturalization of the unmathematical female mind had been so successful and pervasive that, for a long time, historians of mathematics did not even try to understand her work on its own terms, but rather assumed that it was derivative and irrelevant.

Her voice now tells us new and important stories about the age of Enlightenment, the rise of Enlightenment science, and how innovation and tradition are always inextricably linked. Agnesi's life and work illuminate an unexpected intersection of scientific life and religious experience, and the fact that mathematics is necessarily embedded in culture — in fact, it *is* culture. She tells us of a world that we have just begun to explore.

Luchita Hurtado, Untitled, 1977, charcoal on paper, 23 7/8 × 18 7/8 inches
Courtesy the artist and Park View/Paul Soto Los Angeles and Brussels. Photo: Jeff Mclane

YOUTUBE COMMENT #2 TO BJÖRK - SACRIFICE - LIVE @ ZÉNITH DE PARIS, FRANCE, MARCH, 8TH (08-03-2013)

YXTA MAYA MURRAY

Amandapanda 1 minute ago

I am not sure if pregnancy intensifies female rationality or renders it temporarily kaput. As I sit in my bedroom watching YouTube videos of the singer Björk and ponder my future, I am divided on the issue. Finding myself 38 years old, destitute of a lover, making barely more than minimum wage, and still harboring artistic ambition, I must rely on my ability to calculate with mathematical precision various pros and cons when deciding whether to terminate my "condition." Under California law, I have one or two weeks left, and after that I will have to take matters into my own hands, an unreliable and even potentially mortally dangerous prospect. I worry that I am not thinking clearly.

I had never considered motherhood before, a vocation for which I seemed ineligible as a consequence of my devotion to the arts and my fiscal devastation. When I line up these facts on the screen of my computer, the brutal Boolean algebra of the situation = abortion 1, child 0. Abortion true, child false. I have had three previous abortions, procedures that I found arduous but that I endured in order to assign the greatest value to the variable of my art, always my beautiful art, which required from me every single sacrifice. I do not regret this: on account of my choices, I attended RISD and did projects in Japan, Mexico, Chicago, New York, and Rome. I screened a film at Slamdance and I attended Yaddo and I went to MacDowell. I made my calculations, I made my decisions, and so I could do my work.

Yet now, at the age of 38, such logic is overtaken by a delirious vision of a red beating heart filled with love, which has fixated me for the past two weeks. This red beating heart of love does not belong to the fetus but rather to its host, that is, to me. This numinous love courses out of me or perhaps I should say deeper into me. It flows into the seahorse floating within my torso as I write this. This love pulses out of me like blood drops from a wound, and I cannot shrug off the giddy trepidation that Fate or my aging biology calls upon me to nourish my tiny vampire with it until I die.

So you see that I cannot quite understand whether this pregnancy has made me crazy or whether my newfound commitment to self-abnegating love, and its consequent hazards both personal and professional, are symptoms of an infant intelligence that I should not ignore.

Still, I must decide.

※

In the spring of 2013, during her Biophilia Tour, the singer Björk performed before an audience in Paris's Zénith de Paris theater, in the 19th arrondissement. The then-47-year-old avant-garde singer-songwriter appeared in the massive stadium and sang a series of dirges that prayed for technology to reunite human beings with nature, a theme that Björk also illustrated with her choice of costume: a frizzy red wig and a bulbous, off-white dress fashioned of lustrous laser-cut acrylic jersey. This stiff yet undulating armature enveloped her body in what appeared to be a collection of cocoons or navels or sand dunes or anthills. So attired, she wailed the symbolist lyrics of songs like "Sacrifice," which you can play by clicking the arrow above:

Why this sacrifice?
Now she regrets the whole thing,
A delayed reaction.

As Björk sang these lyrics, which could either signify an anthropomorphically warming earth or a disappointed woman, the dress glimmered and protruded on her awkwardly dancing body. The gown was painstakingly crafted by the Dutch designer Iris van Herpen in a 3D manufacturing process that took four months. The costume promoted a particular fantasy for the audience: they weren't just enjoying a concert by an international pop superstar but witnessing the rousings of a human being who had reached an extreme stage of evolution. According to interviews that van Herpen gave to the fashion press, she was inspired by the life cycles of bacilli, vermin, lice, and termites. During the show, the dress's gorgeously creepy biomorphic allusions fused with Björk's lyrical performance. The act presented the crowd with a complex collaboration that drew upon the forceful personalities of the two women artists. Both art forms — the songs, the dress — overlapped and merged until they formed a miraculous composite that sang in different, occasionally clashing registers about the contest between love and death.

Build a bridge to her.
Initiate a touch
Before it's too late.

Björk's lyrics expressed the possibilities of hope and ardor in the face of the apocalypse. Meanwhile, van Herpen's gown glistened like a carapace. The dress raised a skeptical eyebrow at Björk's amorous optimism and seemed, with its lumps and whorls, to confirm the implacable progress of nature, which creates and destroys with terrifying disregard for the human beings it often crushes.

This collaboration and simultaneous competition between the songs and the costume proved a remarkably successful form of aesthetic mutualism. Many artists who work together do not discover such a triumphal resolution to their differences. For example, Mark Rothko found working with Philip Johnson on the Houston Rothko Chapel traumatic. He committed suicide before the chapel was finished. Salvador Dalí and Luis Buñuel worked together on *Un Chien Andalou*, but now Buñuel is the one who gets all of the credit.

Björk and van Herpen's quarrelsome harmony, on the other hand, is delightful precisely because of its dueling messages of faith versus practicality, sympathy versus harsh disinterest.

ᘓᘐ

Iris van Herpen designed Björk's dress with the life cycles of bacilli in mind.

Bacilli develop through a process called sporulation. Bacilli not yet differentiated linger as vegetative cells, and these begin the process of division when they detect certain peptides on their surfaces. The vegetative cells gather nuclear material into filaments, and their plasmatic membrane invaginates, forming a septum. The septum then curves around an immature spore, which develops a double membrane made of the mother cell in a process called engulfment. The spore thereafter grows a cortex called a spore coat, which makes it resistant to heat and solvents. Lysis enzymes then disrupt the mother cell, and the mature spore is released.

What I am describing here is natural subtraction. 1, 0. 1–0=1. That is, the now-invalid mother cell dies while the new spore escapes. Lysis refers to cell disintegration, which occurs when the membrane ruptures. Lysis comes from the Greek word *luein*, which means "loosen."

In a 2007 article published in *The Journal of Bacteriology*, bacteriologists Shigeo Hosoya, Zuolei Lu, Yousuke Ozaki, Michio Takeuchi, and Tsutomu Sato described this stage of spore formation as occurring when the "mother cell engulfs the future daughter cell and eventually actively lyses prior to release of the spore."

They called this the "mother cell death process."

ഗ്ദ

On the Biophilia Tour, why didn't Iris van Herpen's dress engulf the singer Björk and actively lyse? Why didn't Björk find her singing disrupted by Iris van Herpen's spore coat, and begin to asphyxiate from artistically suicidal enzymes?

That is, why did these two beings work together so well and not realize a deadly binary, like Philip Johnson and Mark Rothko, or Luis Buñuel and Salvador Dalí? Why could both be true, and one not demand the falseness of the other?

ഗ്ദ

When I found out I was pregnant 23 weeks ago, I had just quit my demanding job at Snapchat, broken up with my lawyer boyfriend, and started a part-time gig as a salesgirl at Blick, the art-supply store.

In the days before I discovered that I was with child, I had been planning out a performance art piece about white fragility called *Texit*. It's a play that tells the story of a neurotically racist superhero named Texit, who wants Texas to secede from the union because she does not like Mexicans. The afternoon before I took my pregnancy test, I had been making Texit's costume, which involved a lot of blue spandex and a red cape made out of fine Japanese kozogami paper that I had stolen from Blick.

I am a Chicana bisexual performance artist and writer. My life has been about my work. When I saw the two vertical pink lines on my pregnancy test, however, I ceased my labors on Texit.

I am overdue on my rent. I am eating a lot of peanut butter. I have not yet told Brandon, my former boyfriend, about the pregnancy or asked him for money. I do not plan on doing so, either.

I have spent these weeks doing three things:

1) Working at Blick.
2) Crying
3) Writing increasingly personal essays in the comments sections of YouTube, Vimeo, Instagram, Yelp, and Reddit.

ഗ്ദ

In five goddamn minutes I am going to get my act together.

ഊ

Björk Guðmundsdóttir is a single mother. She also holds international renown as a pop-art singer-songwriter. She first achieved fame as the front woman for the band The Sugarcubes, whose biggest hit was the 1987 single "Birthday." Björk's voice sounds weird and warbly and childlike. She has elf eyes and a snub nose. She left The Sugarcubes in the 1990s and embarked upon an almost grotesquely successful solo career, which spans IDM, trip-hop, classical, and electronic musical styles. She dresses crazy in Iris van Herpen bacilli frocks and also wears sexy costumes shaped like swans. She is so famous that in 2015 the Museum of Modern Art in New York held a poorly received retrospective of her work, a show that displayed mainly her music videos.

Björk is a genius. But in 1986, she gave birth to a son named Sindri Eldon Þórsson. Sindri's father was Björk's husband at the time, a guitarist named Þór Eldon. Björk divorced Eldon in 1987 or 1988. In 2000, she became romantically involved with the artist Matthew Barney, and in 2002 bore their daughter, whom they named Isadora "Doa" Bjarkardottir Barney. Björk and Barney broke up in 2013, the same year as Björk's Biophilia Tour. Björk felt so devastated about their estrangement that she wrote a savagely grief-struck album called *Vulnicura*. "Vulnicura" forms a portmanteau of the Latin words for "wound" and "cure," and so means "cure for wounds." The album is really just about the breakup with Matthew Barney, a relationship that had caught on fire and burned down in a bubbling mass of blood and ash.

> From *Vulnicura*'s "History of Touches":
> *I wake you up in the night*
> *Feeling this is our last time together*
> *Therefore sensing all the moments*
> *We've been together.*

Still, all of this warbling about men leaving is not that interesting. Off they go, the men — look at their backsides as they run away. It's not their best angle. Go ahead, sense all the moments, but then go to the bathroom and splash some water on your face. Bye bye, men.

No, the sight of disappearing man-behinds does not prove nearly as fascinating as Björk herself. I find myself fixated particularly on the question of how Björk managed as a single mother to continue making avant-garde work. The babies did not initiate in Björk an artistic mother death process. In 2011, Björk put out a single called "Mother Heroic" where she did sing, "Oh, thou that bowest thy ecstatic face / Thy perfect sorrows are the world's to keep," indicating that parenthood kicked her ass. And in 2015 Matthew Barney sued Björk in the Brooklyn Supreme Court, alleging that Björk monopolized their daughter, Doa. As he testified: "Björk's self-focused mindset [...] flows, in part, from her belief that as Doa's mother, she has far greater rights than I do as Doa's father."

Meanwhile, as Björk jealously clutched her daughter to her hip, she also starred in the badly received show at MoMA and screamed, "I wake you up in the night / Feeling this is our last time together," to packed houses in New York, Manchester, Rome, and Lyon on the Vulnicura Tour. That same year she also released three new videos ("Black Lake," "Family," and "Mouth Mantra"), and an all-string acoustic vinyl of *Vulnicura*, which engaged a viola organista designed in the 15th century by Leonardo da Vinci. She also created an app for her single "Stonemilker" (featuring another grim mothering motif), was nominated for a Grammy, and graced *Time Magazine*'s 100 Most Influential People in the World issue. The newspapers do not report the outcome of the Barney litigation. But in 2016, Björk remained sufficiently artistically liberated that she debuted *Björk Digital*, a virtual reality show that as of this writing travels the globe. She also DJed parties in Australia and Tokyo.

Björk's son is now 31 years old and the leader of his own musical act called Sindri Eldon & the Ways, which is an execrable impersonation of the band Green Day and features Sindri's abysmal nasal singing and insipid guitar playing. "Breaking up is hard to do / But growing up is harder" is the type of stuff Sindri caterwauls into his microphone. Sindri's videos and interviews reveal him as healthy and annoying. He sports a full, glossy beard, indicating that his B12 levels are high; he has obviously not been starved as a result of Björk's artistic single-motherdom. Sindri once told Icelandic Airwaves Journal that he considers himself a far superior lyricist and songwriter than his mother. So, Sindri is frustrated and blames the distaff side as men are wont to do. He is apparently married, though, so perhaps Björk shouldn't be blamed for infecting Sindri with an incurable Hamlet syndrome. All in all, old Sindri appears to be tottering into adulthood in much the same baffled fashion as many other millennials, which is to say, he is doing just fine.

Doa Bjarkardottir Barney is 13 years old. She possesses a Twitter account that lists her home as Brooklyn, where her dad is. So maybe there's some Björk-directed anger there. Doa has 11 followers, and, before she protected her account, she would make public funny fish-eye selfies of herself. She also Tweeted pictures of dogs and of television shows. From this small archive, creepy stalkers/potential artist-mothers doing due diligence could conclude that she has healthy cognitive function. Google Images research reveals that every once in a while paparazzi take pictures of Björk ambling around Iceland hand-in-hand with Doa, so at least they get along well enough to take walks together and physically touch.

It's too soon to tell if Björk's art and possessive personality did any damage to her daughter. I realize that this is a sexist question, but I don't care. I am pregnant and I want to know.

The kid seems normal enough.

As I sit here writing this, I feel nauseated but am trying to ignore it. I am also distracted by a pile of blue and red materials that sits on the work table in the southwest corner of my bedroom. The day I found out I was pregnant, I neatly folded the blue spandex superhero suit and the red kozogami paper super-Texit cape and placed them there. I have not touched them since.

When I began developing *Texit*, I would sit at my desk and write out messy, wonderful drafts of the spoken-word elements and the dancing sections of the show. I planned out how to break the fourth wall and I even designed the lighting, which was inspired by Abe Feder's 1930s designs for the WPA Federal Theater. I would sit almost perfectly still at my table for eight, 10 hours at a time, only taking breaks to drink water and to pee. I would create, drink, and pee. Create, drink, and pee.

I was very "happy," which for an artist means that you are doing the work. It doesn't actually mean that you are what other human beings call happy, which is some sort of emotional state defined by laughing and smiling.

Making art is strange. An artist must trust her outcast nature and not let economics dull her instincts. She must also remain sufficiently remote from personal concerns that she feels free enough to imagine and to execute. I mean, right? I do not know how Björk managed to drop apps and vinyls and get a MoMA show and make the *Time 100* list while hoarding children.

Is it because Björk is rich? On Google it says that Björk's net worth is 45 million dollars, which is exactly 45 million more dollars than I have.

Is it because Iceland has subsidized childcare and six months of guaranteed parental leave?

I am from the United States, which speaks for itself.

Still, other women have been able to simultaneously make art and children without the 45 million and the being from Iceland.

Who again? Karen Finley did it. Toni Morrison has kids. And Sally Mann and Lorna Simpson. Mickalene Thomas.

But let us not forget old Sylvia Plath, who activated an atomic bomb's worth of lysis enzymes on herself when Ted Hughes left her to raise their two children on her own.

☙❧

Iris van Herpen made the shimmering bacilli-themed dress that Björk wore when she took the stage in Paris. The dress enveloped or invaginated Björk but contributed to the performance and did not self-destruct.

Van Herpen is a Dutch designer, aged 33 as I write this. She is tall and rangy with long, dark blonde hair. Her face droops and her wide blue eyes gaze into photographers' lenses with an abstracted expression. She has a boyfriend named Salvador Breed, who works as a sound artist. In 2015, *The New York Times* wrote a profile of van Herpen and illustrated the article with a picture of her and Breed. In the photograph, Breed clings to van Herpen and nuzzles his face into her neck. Van Herpen stares into the middle distance with a slightly disgusted expression. If a meddling wizard froze van Herpen and Breed in those positions and then dragged them apart, Breed would appear to be hugging a ghost and Van Herpen would look as if she were enjoying a solitary moment on a park bench after awakening from an enervating Klonopin high. As far as I can tell from rigorous Google searches, van Herpen does not have any children. She did not breed, or has not yet bred, with Breed.

Van Herpen graduated from the ArtEZ Institute of the Arts Arnhem, in the eastern Netherlands, in 2006. A year later, at the age of 23, she founded her label. Van Herpen quickly grew famous for designing biomorphic science-y outfits that have graced the frames of not only Björk but also Tilda Swinton, Daphne Guinness, and Scarlett Johansson, who are all artists or arty and mothers, as well as incredibly rich.

From the first, Van Herpen made strange dresses that looked like fossils or spaceships. People liked this, but she did not climb toward fashion superstardom until 2010, when she began using 3D printing to make her clothes. Van Herpen was the first designer to bring this technological element into fashion, designing polymer dresses that look like giant dragon mouths and trilobite exoskeletons, or in the case of the Biophilia costume, like anthills and bacilli. *Time Magazine* listed her 3D dresses as one of the 50 best inventions of 2011. Van Herpen attempted a ready-to-wear line but remains most famous for couture. Van Herpen presented at the London and Amsterdam and Paris Fashion Weeks. In 2014, she won the ANDAM Fashion Prize, and in 2015 she won the Marie Claire Prix de la Mode. Her work headlined at the Palais de Tokyo in Paris and the Victoria and Albert in London. In 2012, the Groninger Museum in the Netherlands gave her a solo exhibition, and in 2016, one of her 3D dresses stood next to couture by Yves St. Laurent, Karl Lagerfeld, and Coco Chanel in the Metropolitan Museum of Art's *Manus x Machina* show.

When interviewed, Iris van Herpen does not talk a lot about her boyfriend or her personal plans regarding children. In 2013, however, she did tell Susanne Madsen of *Dazed Magazine* that she loved skydiving. "Skydiving is the most special feeling you can have," she said.

Iris van Herpen is an artist and knows that she must remain free.

Luchita Hurtado, *Untitled*, c. 1976, charcoal on paper, three parts, each: 14 × 10 5/8 inches
Courtesy the artist and Park View/Paul Soto Los Angeles and Brussels. Photo: Jeff Mclane

ജ്ഞ

In the video "Sacrifice," Björk stands beneath a spotlight and sings, "Build a bridge to her," while Iris van Herpen's dress flashes like a wasp's nest around her body.

Björk and Iris van Herpen do not activate murderous enzymes against themselves or each other during this interaction. Instead, the singer and the dress debate each other. Their main disagreement seems to be about the ability of the human race to feel and give love during the ghastly age of the Anthropocene. Björk insists that such human love remains possible, but the dress suggests that Björk perseveres only because she is a predator, as all humans are predators who seek the tragic paradox of sporification and survival.

Through their work, these two women also initiate a conversation about loneliness and art. When Björk sings about building a bridge she claims that the female artist doesn't have to be isolated. She can be connected with the rest of the world. Meanwhile, van Herpen's dress, which encases Björk like armor or a habitat, suggests something quite different: the artist may long for love but, alas, can exist only in the self-sustaining microcosm that is her work.

The observer, however, may note excitedly that both ideas persist despite their contradictions. Björk does not trigger lysis in van Herpen and van Herpen does not rupture Björk. In this universe, Johnson does not kill Rothko and Buñuel spares Dalí. There is no horrid Boolean loosening. There are, instead: Morrison, Finley, Thomas, Simpson, and Mann. Life flourishes in the struggle between love and the pitiless labor of creation.

"Sacrifice" suggests a dazzling idea: the affectionate cannibal, who is also an artist, need not fear subtraction. The red beating heart filled with love + art = a possibility.

ജ്ഞ

This is what I mean by wondering whether pregnancy elevates reason or renders a formerly rational person totally nutty.

Perhaps I should not be getting family planning and career advice from YouTube.

My body swells like a fruit. I look to the southwest corner of my bedroom and wonder how the superhero Texit costume would look on me at eight months. Pretty good, I think.

If I went back to my old job at Snapchat and, realistically, accepted a year off from art, I might be able to manage it.

Snapchat salary = $65k before tax. Hours = ~ 60. Hours in a week = 168. Hours spent sleeping = 49. 45? 40?

Rent = $30k. Childcare in Los Angeles, approx. annual cost = ~ $14.5k

ꙮ

What if you have a child and take a year off from art and then discover you can't do it anymore?

Mother cell death? Now she regrets the whole thing, a delayed reaction.

Or maybe you just make the art, even if you can't. You sing about love and bridges at the same time that you wear the terrifying dress.

Art 1, Child 0.

Art 0, Child 1.

Art 1, Child 1.

ꙮ

Art 1, Child 1.

The real problem is the money.

THE FAMILY GENIUSES

ZEYNEP KAYHAN

It was February 1991, and I was in the schoolyard with Begüm and Merve, playing elastics. For weeks I'd been practicing at night in the laundry room, with my brother, who was then a little over three, standing on one end of the rubber band and an old Thonet chair on the other. We kept the TV on, flipping back and forth between a smirking Bruce Willis in *Moonlighting* and the kryptonite night-vision of Operation Desert Storm. Then as now, I was wily but lacked strength; I never got the crisscrosses right.

But that day, out in the cold in my scratchy petrol blue uniform and knee-high socks for peak performance, I found myself entering a flow state. I jumped the English round, zero contact, breezed through the second level with the width of the loop reduced down to a single ankle. The scissors too started off well. I was too slow, too cautious to be a natural. Still I'd caught the rhythm of the thing, felt my ponytail whipping my shoulders at a satisfying beat.

A boy from a grade up stopped by to watch. A week earlier, on Valentine's Day, he'd given me a pretty gift-wrapped package which turned out to contain a single monstrous cucumber. Hand in pocket, he tugged on the rubber band with his foot and let it bounce back. "I think you should know," he murmured, "They're beating up your brother in the boys' bathroom."

Immediately, I thought of my brother's head. It was a large head, but not unattractive, with a smooth elongated high curve at the back. In those days my mother was having it shaved in the style of the NATO officers who lived in our apartment building. They were big red men with icy glares and dowdy wives. On their military-grade shoulders, the close side shave telegraphed unwavering purpose. On a three-year-old it exposed an odd, tenacious vulnerability. On the occasions when my brother drifted off to sleep in the car on our way back from school, I'd divert my eyes from the head's precarious wobble.

Recently, I'd been made privy to the head's new and mysterious abilities. At breakfast one morning, I'd overheard my brother telling our nanny to stop checking the papers for news of her long-lost son. "Your boy is dead," he told her. "Better you accept it."

When dear nanny gave him a look of pained incomprehension, he repeated his prognosis in brisk *CNN* English. A few days after that, he snuck into my room to inflict his daily share of low-level disturbance. I was busy memorizing the names of sugar factories in Middle Anatolia for a geography test. From the corner of my eye, I could see him peering at the world map that hung above my desk. He hesitated briefly, then pushing aside a pile of mistreated Barbies pointed to the country next to ours and exclaimed with inscrutable joy, "Iraq!"

"Syria!" he cried out a little later, eyes widening. He moved his chubby finger a little to the right. "Iran!"

He paused there for a bit, tracing the borders, letting that heavy name sink in. Then the finger abruptly pointed down: "Kuwait! Kuwait!"

He mimed explosion sounds and performed a demented, primitive, sugar-high dance around my bedroom, stopping every now and then to name-check another luckless land off the map. He was determined to finish off the Middle East once and for all.

At school, more than anywhere else, the point is to be serious about violence. Still, as I ran up the stairs to save the head, to stop it from getting smashed to a pulp on the filthy floors of a public school toilet, my stomach churned. It was exhausting, having to fight boys every day.

ﻫ

I was at my grandmother's house going through the contents of her bedside table, when I came upon an odd postcard. On one side was a picture of a milk coronet rising out of a gleaming red surface. The postcard had been sent to my grandmother in 1961 by her only remaining brother, a professor of electrical engineering at MIT. She'd lost her other brothers, in quick succession, to myriad 20th-century accidents. One of them had crashed his glider plane, the other had gone under in a scuba diving tragedy, and the youngest had run his motorcycle into a laundry truck.

The surviving brother had addressed the first part of the postcard to my mother, aged one at the time.

"Dear Niece," he wrote. "Here in Cambridge, we've overcome time. We've overcome God." A mind-numbing passage followed, detailing various advancements in flash technology, high-frequency transistors and semiconductors.

The second part was addressed to my grandmother, and dealt in personal matters.

"I've met a beautiful girl," the great-uncle wrote. "She has complete heterochromia like a Van cat, and studies at the nursing school." But he was worried. The girl suffered from stomach ulcers and drank three bottles of milk a day to ease her symptoms.

"Do you think, dear sister, that in middle-to-old age she will be very fat?"

We laughed and laughed. We rolled over on the carpet. Tears streamed from our eyes. Our heads throbbed.

"What can you do," my grandmother said gasping for breath. "He's the genius!"

VIBRANT ISLANDS

JAAP BLONK

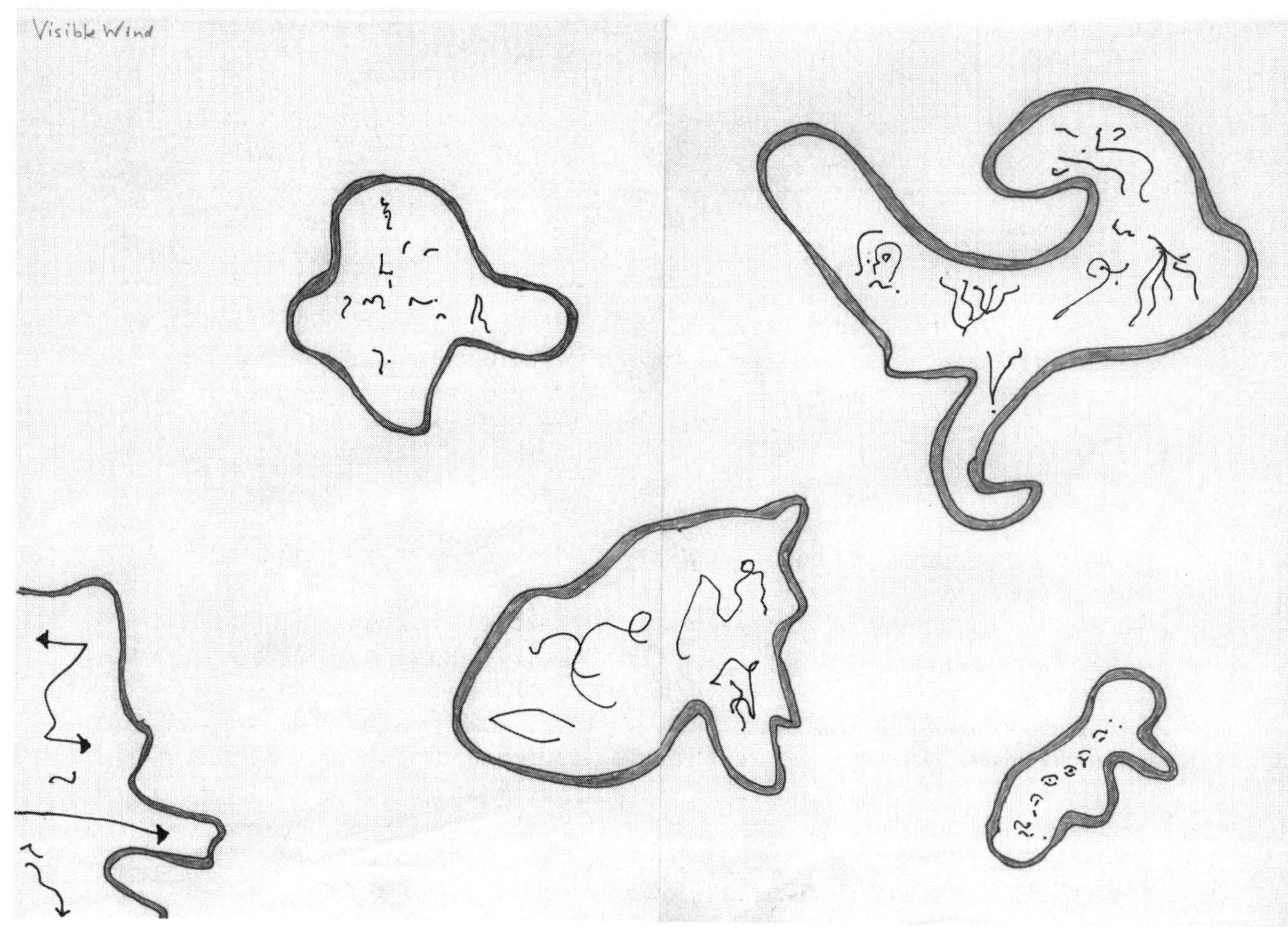

Visible Wind, 2015

Vibrant Islands is a cycle of nine pieces, a visual score for acoustic vocal performance, made in 2015. Each movement consists of a number of "islands" containing phonetic signs, many of which were invented. In the performance the islands can be visited repeatedly and in any order. In every score of the cycle the coastal lines have a different form i.e. angular, crenelated, straight or rounded, according to the prevalent sound character of the movement. The language used here is part of Blonk's personal extension of the International Phonetic Alphabet: BLIPAX (BLonks IPA eXtended).

A complete performance of "Vibrant Islands" can last between 36 and 63 minutes.

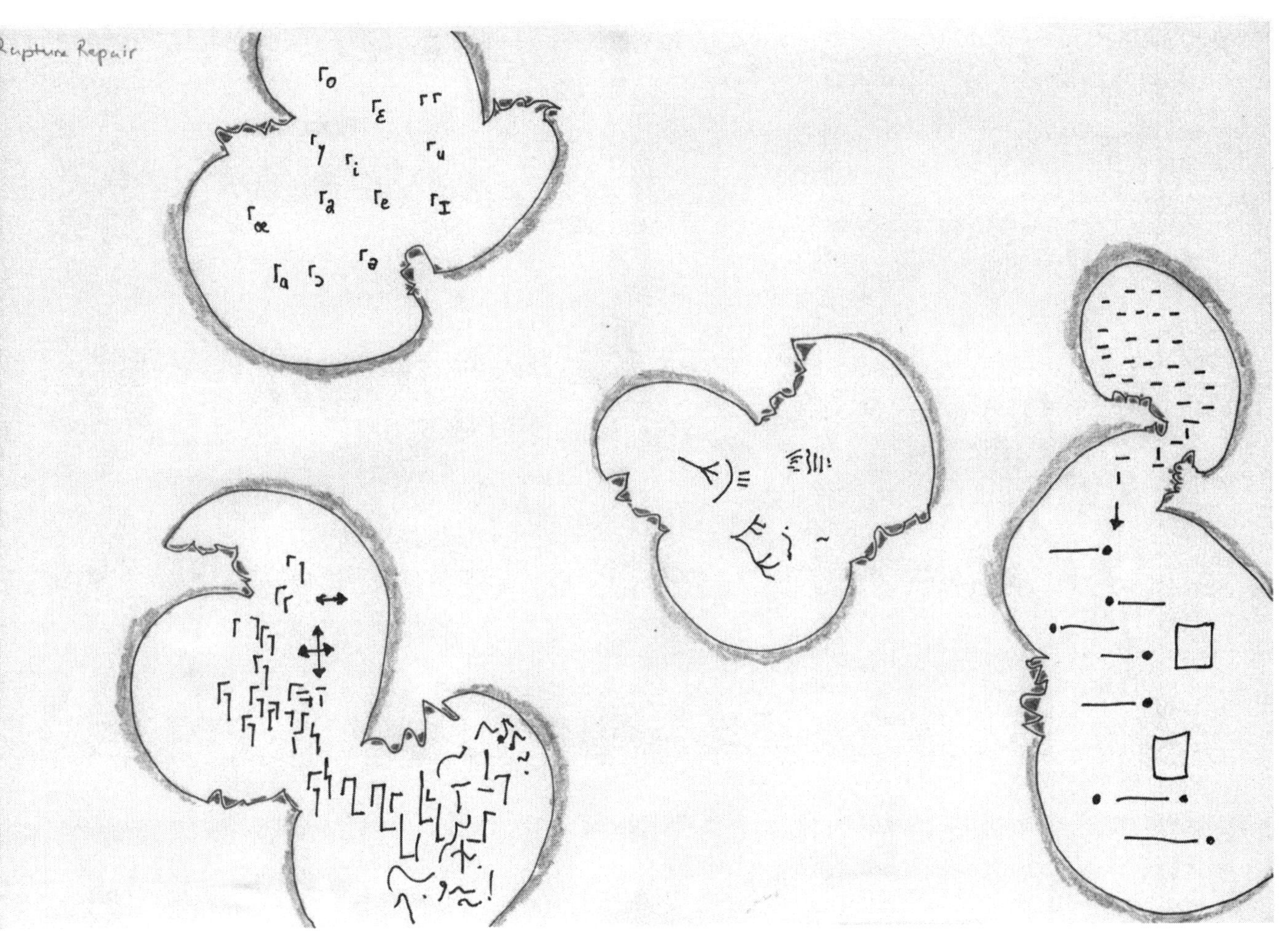

Rupture Repair, 2015

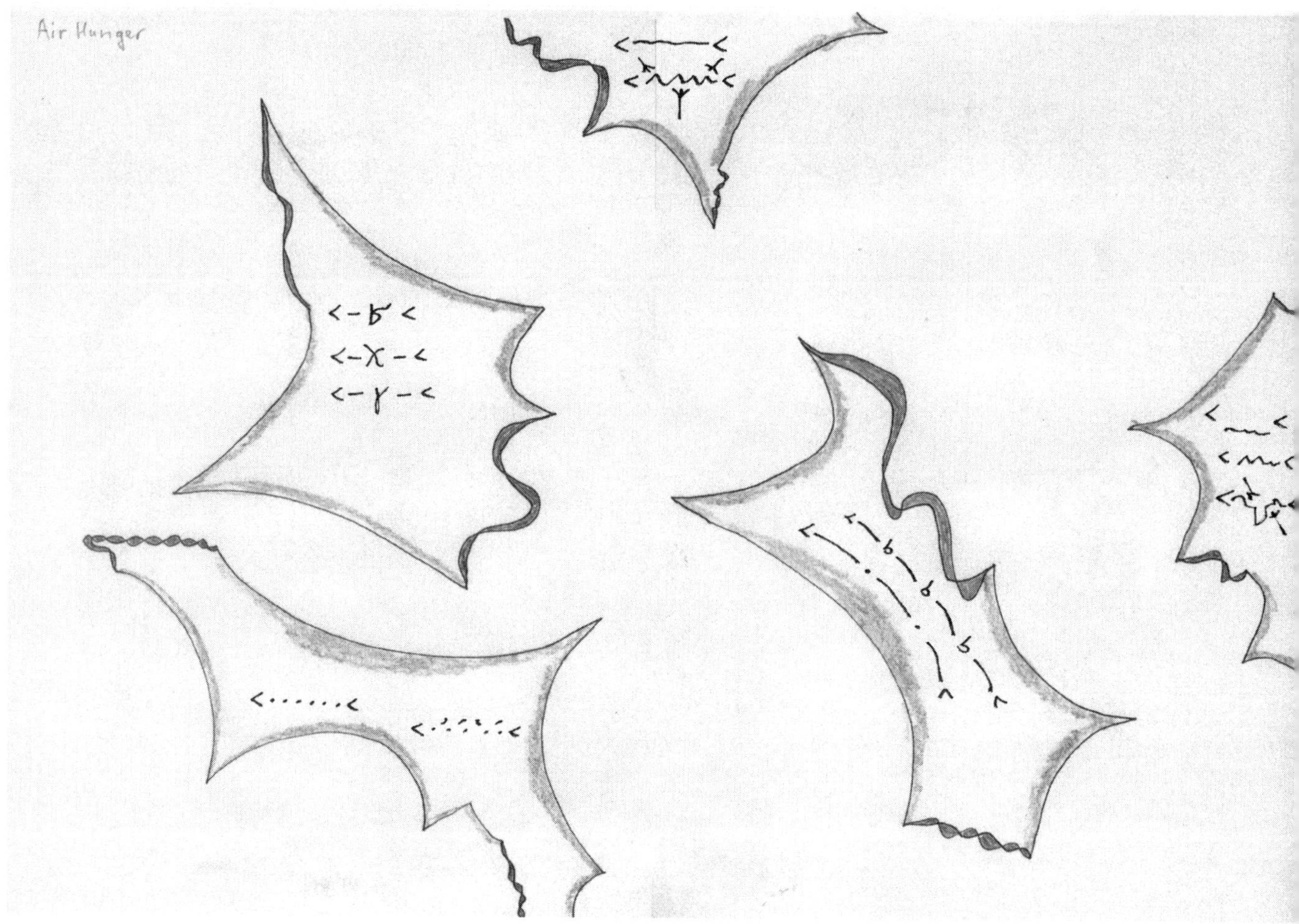

Jaap Blonk, *Air Hunger*, 2015

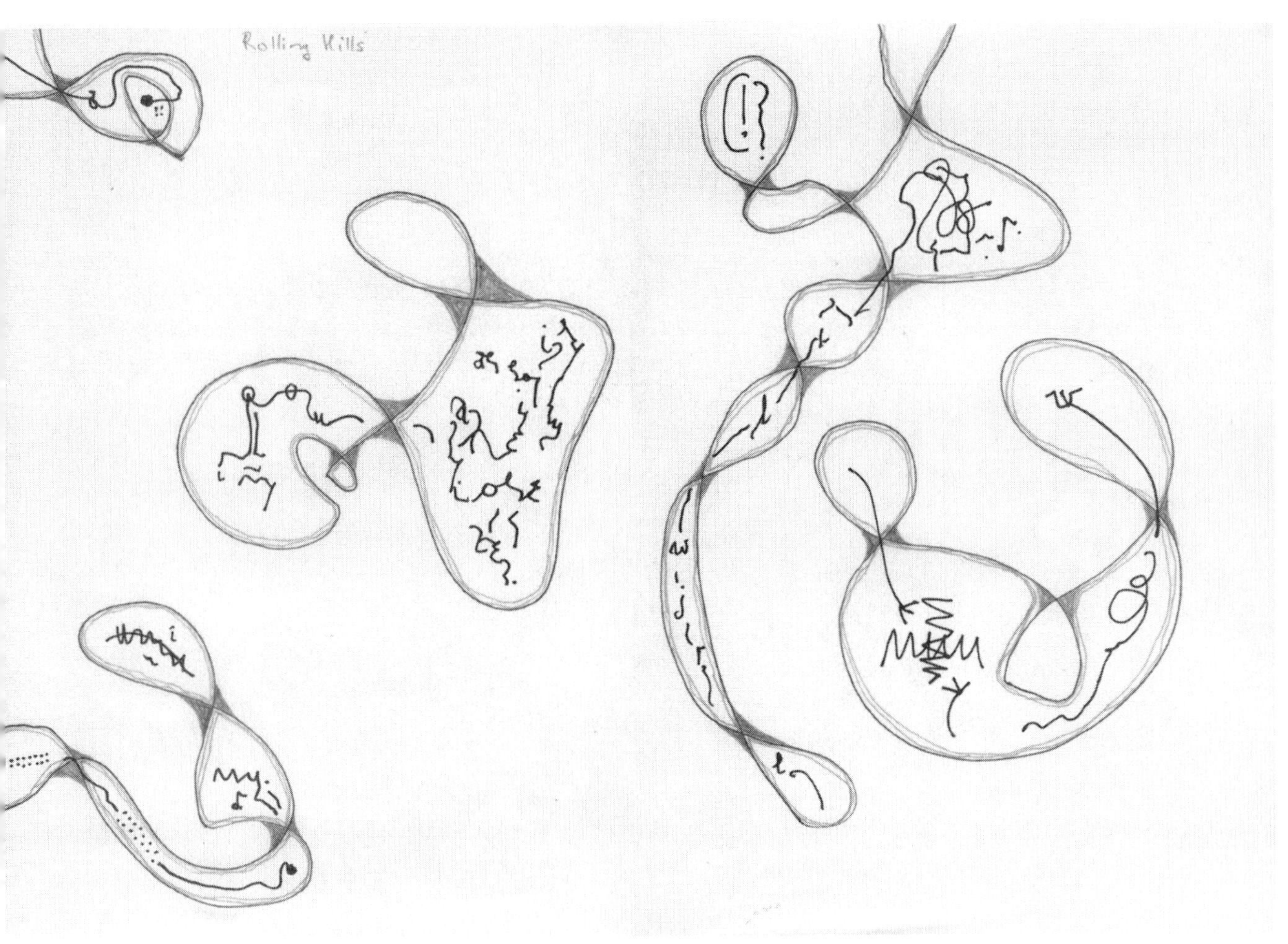

Jaap Blonk, *Rolling Hills*, 2015

MARINA IN NERVI

DAVID YEZZI

My father called that place our paradise:
that was its name, the Golfo Paradiso—
with olive trees, high cactuses and palms,
quince threes in December, bougainvillea
growing riot on the schist along the coast,
orange-glow pyracantha, butcher's-broom,
and sunlight in the morning on the mountains.
I couldn't wait to leave it. Why was that?
Today, it seems a precious memory.
My sin was squandering, and now I'm being
punished for my sin. I've been cast out.

O little girl, my one light, my Irina,
what did I do to you? How very cold
you must have been. It hurts to think of it—
so hungry all the time, so very hungry,
the pain of it eating daily at your limbs,
your thought when you woke up, your midnight thought
that barely let you sleep. Your body ached
until there was not food enough to feed
the tiny flutter of your heart or fill
your lungs. I thought the orphanage would feed you,
but you died on a cot in a freezing corridor.
Io non piangëa, sì dentro impetrai.
And then we starved, and Moscow was our prison.

For two nights I have dreamt about the sea,
the *pensione* below the Apennines,
the switchback paths that took us to the beach.
I was a girl, like you, though I was older.
The hotelier's son was my age and so quiet.
I never spoke to him, but we would catch
each other's eyes whenever he was working
in the garden where we children took our breakfast
or on the pavements overgrown with succulents.
His talent was for painting. He had learned
the trompe-l'oeil style they practice in that region.
From my window I would watch him on a scaffold
restoring to the stucco pale cornices,
faux curtains blowing out of open shutters,
all make believe, ascribing depth to flatness
with his brush. That summer, I believe, I loved him,
just puppy love—though still I think of him.
He was an artisan of considerable skill,
no writer, thank god. I loved him more for that.
Heaven has room for gifted artisans,
but poets, for their sins, are rarely saved.
So much the better, Mother liked to say.

Poor Mother was the reason we had gone
to winter in Liguria. Her health was bad,
Her doctor recommended a milder climate,
clear air and sun. Then, Nervi was a spa,
with villas in the overhanging hills
and the passeggiata like a beached leviathan,
where I would wheel her in her rattan chair,
with blankets heaped up on her lap and scarves
around her neck and set her in the sun.
Tucked in against the cliff-face, she would sit
for hours with the villagers and tourists,
basking in the hothouse of the low light
and counting as the little fishing boats
went out and came back past the rocky breakwater.
And dogs on leashes leapt to meet their friends,
whose owners brought them each day without fail,
so that we learned their names—Allegro, Jacquie.
In her flowing layers underneath the palms
she looked like a grand dame out of Matisse,
and for a while we could forget her illness,
though her pale face always told a different story.

And when the winds came unexpectedly
that autumn, we all kept inside. I heard
the rattle of the great French doors
that opened on my bedroom balcony
rumble and thud as if the wind had made
them angry to be bolted shut all day.
And through the shaking glass I watched with awe
the giant palm tree bend as if to break
and in a lull come to itself again
until, frightened by its violent back and forth,
I had to look away. Then came the rain.
I remember in Camogli how the surf
churned up the beach of polished, palm-sized stones
each time it drew back, and the sound it made
was of bed linens slowly torn for bandages
by nurses who are caring for the wounded.
But then after a week or so the sun
would find me out where I had squirreled away
on the divan in the dim parlor or in bed,
and lure me out of doors in the dying breeze
and up the chalky cliffside, clambering.
On clear days, when the sun shone on the sea
like the momentary blinding of a flashbulb,
I felt happy. The grand houses and hills
seemed new-born as if scrubbed clean of their demons.

But you can't eat the landscape, nor can memories
of pleasant days sustain you longer than
a sudden reverie in which the book
your holding drops beside your chair, the pages
splaying out like a vision of the sea
as it occludes your thoughts of pain with its narcotic.
Worn off again, they all come crashing back
like the incessant waves, the rush and cry of spume,
threading through the rocks and surging up
in plumes of spray then falling back again
into the vast, engulfing, unopposable ocean.

These days we rarely see the sun,
your sister and I. And the cleansing light,
which made me feel the world had been redeemed,
here serves merely to shine a light on Hell,
its recesses and obscure depths, which delve
more deeply than I ever knew was possible.
We ate the horses.

In dreams these past two nights, I saw myself
walking the passeggiata with my eyes
cast down, combing the paving stones to find
a button that had fallen from the bodice
of my dress close my heart. It must have popped
when I was chasing Jacquie and Allegro.
How foolish I was to wear my new clothes
to play with dogs. I hoped the owner's boy—
what was his *name*?—might like to see me in them.
I never think of dresses now, but then
it was my favorite possession.
And stupidly I ruined everything.
I seethed and cursed myself, and I cursed God
for taking from me what I loved the best.
The secrets of my future happiness
were layered in those whorls of nacreous
pearl, my fingers fumbling with them each morning,
as I looked out over the charcoal ocean.
Vanished. Lost. Gone for good—an odd expression.
Then after an hour of walking and hot tears—
crying, cursing, stomping back and forth—
I found it glinting in a patch of sunlight,
as if that single shaft had guided me
to it, my good thing, mine again, returned.
That day I could believe in answered prayers.
Our nanny teased me, sewing it back on,
and by dinner it was as if I'd never lost it.

O idiot, you hopeless idiot.

It's funny I should think about that now.
It seems as if it happened to a stranger.
How far away that coast is and that girl.
You hear the church bell? Is it there or here,
clanging the hour in Saint-Sulpice? It's hot.
The caged electric fan mimics the slow,
incessant churning of water on the rocks,
that day the tempest overturned the lampposts,
and piled the little harbor with debris.
The villagers came out, as after a shipwreck,
smiling amazedly at the rough water,
grateful for the sunlight peeking through
the fuchsia clouds above the quieting sea.
I wish that you had been there, my Irina.
Surely, I'll never see that place again.

Paris 1926

A SPLENDID HISTORY: HENRY LOUIS GATES JR. ON AFRICA'S ANCIENT CIVILIZATIONS

SCOTT TIMBERG

Henry Louis Gates Jr. has been a leading scholar and critic of black history and literature since he published The Signifying Monkey *30 years ago, now a classic of literary criticism. More recently, Gates, who has taught at Harvard since 1991, has thrived as an interpreter in the Carl Sagan model: he has hosted the PBS ancestry series* Finding Your Roots, *and a number of documentaries, like the six-hour series* Africa's Great Civilizations.

Here, Gates discusses our perceptions of Africa, the narratives that shape these perceptions, and the many ancient civilizations that thrived around the continent.

ꕥ

SCOTT TIMBERG: Do you ever ask yourself, "What do the people I'm talking to already know about Africa? Where is our common starting ground?" For so long, Africa has been the subject of stereotyping, misconception, and willful misinterpretation.

HENRY LOUIS GATES JR.: Unfortunately, Africa was a tabula rasa and on it was inscribed the worst stereotypes from the subconscious of the Western human community. For centuries, Africa has been associated with poverty, disease, corruption, and even more importantly, the word "undeveloped." It appeared in Hegel's *Philosophy of History* in 1837 when he wrote about Africa. Historian Hugh Trevor-Roper used the same word in an infamous essay published in 1965. Meaning, there was no movement or change in the terms people used to talk about the continent. If you went a thousand years back, people were living in mud houses and, you know, attempting to make crops grow, and their descendants 10 generations later were living in the same mud houses. Africa was portrayed as static, undeveloped, "primitive."

On one hand, that is an ideal situation [for a documentarian] but of course, it's unfortunate for Africa. We all learned these ideas from the media and TV. Not just white people but black people too! All of us got our images of Africa from *Tarzan*.

I was born in 1950. Wouldn't I have learned from *Ramar of the Jungle* and *Tarzan* and *Sheena, Queen of the Jungle*? Not to mention, *National Geographic*, which was also slightly pornographic.

You mean that Africa was presented as a continent in a permanent state of inertia.

A permanent state of undiscovery until white people showed up. This is Dr. Livingstone's work, who was one of the first white people to penetrate the interior of Africa — over in Southeast Africa — because he was looking for the source of the Nile. In fact, the origin of the human community began in Africa, when anatomically modern human beings walked out of the continent some 80,000 to 50,000 years ago. The first writing is also from Africa, as well as the first forms of visual art. Painting! The Blombos Cave [in South Africa] is an amazing example — the paintings there are from 80,000 years ago. We even found the palette.

All the stuff that we thought had come first — the French caves for example — forget it. It first came from Africa 80,000 years ago. The first iron technology in the world came from Africa in 1800 BC. Ceramic technology followed. That was 11,500 years ago. Cotton textile weaving in Sudan — 5000 BC. It developed at the same time as India or slightly after India. That's amazing!

Africa was also in touch with the rest of the world from the very beginning. Africans have been trading with each other and with the outside world from time immemorial. Most of Europe's gold, between 1000 and 1500 — the Middle Ages and the latter Middle Ages, the beginning of the Renaissance — actually came from West Africa. People don't know that. The Sahara Desert, the Red Sea, the Nile, the Congo River, the Indian Ocean were highways. They didn't separate Europe, Saudi Arabia, Persia, India, China from Africa. They linked them to it.

In fact, the second nation in the world to become Christian was Ethiopia in 350 AD. When Prince Lorenzo de' Medici is being educated [in Milan], around the 15th century, he is taught the names of the four or five great world leaders. The king of the Kongo, Álfonso I, is on that list. When the Portuguese finally arrive in Kongo, in 1483, the king of Kongo willingly converts to Roman Catholicism and converts his whole kingdom by 1491. He then has his son educated in Europe, in Portugal. The pope later makes the king's son, Henrique, the first bishop in the Kingdom of Kongo in 1517.

Can you tell us a little more about African history? Does Africa stand at the beginning of human culture?

Oh, yeah. We can start 200,000 years ago with mitochondrial DNA — unfortunately, we don't know the identities of these people. If we jump in time, to about 3000 BC, we have Egypt and Nubia. Nubia includes the Kingdoms of Kush and Kerma. Moving south, there was the Kingdom of Kerma, then city-state of Napata, then Meroë, which was the capital city of the Kingdom of Kush. All of these civilizations continued down into the Christian neighborhoods [in Ethiopia]. And then we have the Kingdom of Aksum.

Actually, there's a book written in Greek in 50 AD, which is basically a TripAdvisor guide to sailing down the Red Sea. It first directs you to the port, called Adulis, which is in the Kingdom of Aksum in Eritrea. This book describes the king, tells you what you can trade, what you can get, and what you should bring. Written in Greek in 50 AD!

In 25 BC, Meroë, which was part of Nubia, was ruled by a black queen named Amanirenas — she was the *Kandake* [Meroitic term for "queen"]. She defeated the Romans! She took three cities, each of which is Roman by this time. She captured and confiscated a statue of Augustus Caesar and buried it in front of her throne back in Meroë, so that everybody who came to see her had to step on Augustus Caesar. [*Laughs.*] The name Candace actually derives from the *Kandake*, queen of Meroë — a totally black kingdom. How come people don't know these stories?

How did Egypt relate to these other kingdoms?

Egypt and Nubia were Janus figures, connected by the Nile. They crossed; they exchanged goods — Egypt's gold came from the Kingdom of Kush. They also fought each other.

In the first volume of *Image of the Black in Western Art*, which I co-edited with David Bindman, there are Egyptian representations of Nubians, and they're always represented darker. We don't know what the Egyptians looked like, but we know that they represented the Nubians in a more "African" kind of way. But the Nubians would have been a mixed-race people, of course they were. The reason that we have these negative images of Africa is that they were invented to justify the slave trade.

Europeans did this too, of course. European philosophers — Hume in 1754, Kant in 1764, Jefferson in 1785, Hegel in 1837 in *Philosophy of Discourse* — they all wrote about Africa to justify the slave trade. I was just reading this on the plane actually: Hegel actually took Egypt out of Africa. He wrote, Egypt, that's not really Africa!

There were also a lot of white people in Africa, [Saint] Augustine's people for example or Tertullian. These men were the early fathers of the church from Northern Africa. When the Berbers and the Almoravids took over the Iberian Peninsula, they had a mixed-race army, so there were also lot of black people among the moors. There were the moors and the blackamoors.

You've gotten into trouble for talking and writing about the slave trade in the past and the issue comes up in this PBS documentary series on Africa. The slave trade was of course mostly run by Europeans and Americans, but there were also black West Africans who were a part of it. How significant were they?

John Thornton and Linda Heywood, two of the most prominent African historians, were consultants on this series. They teach at Boston University. They tell me that about 90 percent of the Africans sold in the slave trade to the New World were captured and sold by African merchants to Europeans along the coast.

When I was growing up, the stories were often: Your ancestors were out for a picnic on a Sunday and some white man jumped out of the bushes with a net. In fact, it wasn't really like that. It was business — a huge business unfortunately.

What do you think this tell us about human nature and about history?

It tells us that the African elites who profited from the slave trade were human — all too human, just like everybody else. But we constructed a narrative of innocence in order to protect ourselves from dealing with the horror of one of our black ancestors selling other black people. In all fairness, though, they didn't see each other as black. They were members of kingdoms or tribes: the Yoruba as opposed to the Ibo, for example.

When we talk about African culture or artistry — sculpture, cave-painting, figurines, music — what was culture to people? Was it status? Was it being part of a group identity? Was it honoring the gods?

I think culture was a way of making sense out of your existence. I think that's part of what unites us with our ancestors — the Blombos Cave and the art-making impulse. It's also what distinguishes us from other animal life, our ability for second-order reflection. We have the capacity to do something and reflect on the doing of that thing. We have that in common with our ancestors — even the earliest ancestors out of Africa.

One form that reflection took was visual — painting. But, it took other forms as well — writing and music, a sense of irony.

All of those things developed in the human community…I believe we can't help it. We can't help but reflect on what we do. Unlike other members of what we used to call the animal kingdom, we act and we reflect on our actions. That's what's different about us.

You recently published a volume on African-American folktales. Can you talk about the connection between African culture and American art?

It is clear that the slaves, despite the horrors of the Middle Passage, brought their cultures with them and that out of the many African cultures was born a new African-American culture, with roots tracing back to the various cultures of West and West Central Africa. A classic example is the Anansi trickster tales, which originated among the Akan people in what is today Ghana.

There were also the Flying African tales. These tales took two forms: in one type, enslaved Africans, upon arrival in the New World, refused to be enslaved, and, in one way or another, flew off to Africa. In the other form, Africa was the place where the souls of the enslaved returned, to spend eternity in paradise. I find that idea charming, and so uplifting. My co-editor, Maria Tatar, and I dedicated an entire section of the book to these Flying African tales.

One of the fascinating things about the film *Black Panther* is the vision of the nation of Wakanda, a kingdom somehow simultaneously folkloric and futuristic. It's a country without poverty, disease, or much impact from white people, including colonialism or slavery. Of course, it's fictional, but maybe no more "constructed" than the image of Africa most of us have been taught over the years. How did this utopian imagining of an African nation strike you? Does it feel like a country that almost might have been?

I saw *Black Panther* twice; I loved the movie. The truth is that any time this many people around the world are thinking about Africa in a positive light — that is certainly to be celebrated.

But at the same time, I have to wonder: Why it is so much easier to identify with a utopian fantasy of Africa than the reality of contemporary Africa — or the realities of the splendid history of the African past, the very history of civilization in Africa?

osite page: Brian Randolph, *Breathing Page*, 2017, pen and pencil on paper, 21 x 14 3/4 inches

BEHIND THE MOON

ANOSH IRANI

Abdul was too tired to chase the rat. Perhaps the rat knew, Abdul thought, because it wasn't trying to run. It moved slowly, inch by inch, along the base of the small refrigerator where Abdul kept his Cokes and Sprites. Whenever a customer left some in the can, he would bring them to his tiny room at the back of the restaurant. At the end of the day, he would empty them into two separate one-liter bottles — Cokes in one, Sprites in the other. It reminded him of how he used to steal petrol from motorcycle tanks when he was young, sucking the fuel through a pipe until it burned the tip of his tongue, only to let it stream into a plastic bottle. But that seemed like a lifetime ago, in Bombay. He had no use for petrol now. Ever since he had come to Canada, he only sat on the bus. And stared out the window into what wasn't his nation.

The rat was really thin. It had now moved past the refrigerator, and toward Abdul's clothing rack. The one good coat Abdul possessed was given to him by his owner upon Abdul's arrival to Vancouver five years ago. It had felt so soft and elegant back then, but had very quickly revealed itself for what it truly was — a shield against the rain and snow. It wasn't a piece of clothing; it was something you put on when you were under attack. And the gray woolen fibers that Abdul had put against his face on that first night in Vancouver, which he mistook for a kind hand, a welcoming touch, now seemed repelling. The rat was made of that same wool, that same color. If his owner saw Abdul just staring at the rodent, not doing a damn thing about it, he would lose his mind. Qadir Bhai was kind as long as you listened to him. At this moment, his instructions would be: "Abdul, kill that bloody thing." And he would be right. A rat had no place in the Mughlai Moon. It was a place for lamb and kebabs. As a cook in the restaurant, how could Abdul allow the rat even a single breath? But Abdul couldn't kill it. That rat had found a way in but could not find a way out. That rat was him.

Abdul could feel the nausea rising within, brought upon him by his new country. He was a passport-less creature; he had used a tourist visa to enter Canada, and was now one of the invisibles. The food that he cooked each day for the Mughlai Moon was the only sign of his existence, but that too disappeared — and rightly so, he felt — into the bellies of taxi drivers, construction workers, security guards, and janitors, to remind Abdul that he was digestible, someone the system chewed and shat out. He was no immigrant. His Indian passport was with Qadir Bhai, in an apartment with carpets and Netflix. His passport had better living conditions than he did. Qadir Bhai kept it for "safekeeping," alongside loads of cash that he never declared, cash made from Abdul's food, from Abdul's sweat. Once, when the immigration authorities had come to quiz Qadir Bhai about Abdul's whereabouts, Abdul was only a few feet away. He was about to clear a customer's plate when he saw the two men and smelled an air of authority. So he just sat down at the table and started eating from that same plate, used his hands on someone else's leftover chicken, pretending to be a customer. He had lost his hair, he had lost his weight, he was no longer the 25-year-old who bristled with energy, so there was little chance of him being recognized from his passport photo. He was tired, and with tired, trembling eyes he sat there and watched as the men grilled Qadir Bhai, who said with the confidence of a seasoned actor, "That fellow is gone. He has run away. I brought him here to visit this beautiful city, as a favor to his parents. He has shamed me and my family. I had no idea he would do this." When the customer next to him got up to leave, Abdul skulked away too.

It unnerved him how easy it was for Qadir Bhai to speak an untruth.

Abdul's parents had been dead for a long time and Qadir Bhai had never even met them. When Qadir Bhai spoke those words, Abdul wanted to reveal himself to the authorities just so that he could clear his name and tell them that he had been tricked by Qadir Bhai, who had promised him that he was "legal." But what good would that have done? Abdul would have been too terrified to speak in his broken English, words that he had picked up here and there, scraps of a new language that had been thrown at him as though he were a beggar.

How he envied the men who ate his food — they had managed to acquire a Canadian accent, and when they ate his food with their bare hands, broke a piece of naan and dipped it in their dal, their bruised knuckles showed, their calluses showed. These were honest calluses; Abdul had burns from stoves and frying pans and cooking oil — his were not badges of honor, they were marks of shame and punishment. The men who ate his food held Canadian passports and roamed the streets freely while he was forced to hide in a room at the back of a restaurant. "If anyone asks, you live in someone's basement in Abbotsford," Qadir Bhai had told him. Then he handed Abdul a frayed piece of paper: "Just memorize this address." So once, on Abdul's day off, he caught the bus to his fake address and saw how beautiful it was.

But everyone could smell a rat.

Especially in a restaurant, where the aroma of food was what drew people in to begin with. Which is why, perhaps, no one ever questioned him. One night, when the "M" of the Mughlai Moon almost fell off, and Abdul had to repair it, it occurred to him what his real address was.

I live behind the moon, he thought. And it made his tiny room feel a bit warmer.

Unlike now.

His breathing was getting heavier and heavier. It had to come every now and then — that sinking feeling — and it came without warning. As though someone had taken dusk and poured it down his throat. His heart was pounding, his hands were cold. It was that same boring feeling of regret and anger, a deep realization of impotence, which brought him to his knees. Before he came to this country, the only time he fell to his knees was during *namaz*: his surrender to Allah was a glorious one, so magnificent it had the scent of roses and the taste of sherbet in it. When he prayed in Bombay, he got down on his knees out of sheer gratitude. Here, he fell; he was beaten into submission, a sick *mareez* looking to the sky for help. But there was no sky, just the cold gray paint of the ceiling above. Everything was gray, everything was rat.

He knew he had to snap out of this.

He went to where his clothes were placed. It was a shell of a cupboard, a hollow space without a door, a gift from Qadir Bhai's university-educated son who had destroyed the cupboard in a fit of anger, and had then given it to Abdul as an act of charity. The empty hooks that were tacked to the upper panel reminded Abdul of the chickens that used to hang from hooks at the slaughterhouse in Bombay where he worked, where he taught his brother Hasan, 15 years younger than him, how to skin the animals and cut through bone without making a mess. To think that he preferred the sight of dead animals to the gray woolen coat that hung — like a man was already in it, a very thin man, extremely still, afraid to move.

Behind the coat stood his cricket bat.

He grabbed the handle, felt the rubber grip against his palm. He wasn't going for the rat, but the rat suddenly sizzled with energy and bolted off. Abdul didn't bother to trace it. He felt the wooden surface of the bat. It smelled of linseed oil. There were red marks on it, marks that he cherished because they were signs of victory, like when his team needed six runs off the final ball to win the league, and Abdul pulled a shot out of nowhere — or so it seemed to the rest of the team — and won the match. Ten of his teammates holding their breath, then exhaling with joy. But things changed the minute he got off the cricket field; the only time anyone held their breath for him was because he stank of food.

His thoughts were getting the better of him tonight. He couldn't understand why. These were winter thoughts. These were thoughts that came with rain. The night was dry, and winter was over. He told himself that all he had to do was get through the night. Tomorrow was his day off. A Sunday. Tomorrow was the beginning of the cricket season.

He held on to the bat tighter, but all it did was make him sweat more, so he kept it back in its place. He rolled out his mattress and switched off the light. In the dark, he imagined what being Canadian would feel like: to be able to sit at Tim Hortons and have a donut without feeling like a thief; to walk along the sea wall in Stanley Park and not view the sea as an endless extension of lost hopes and dreams; to be able to ride in a taxi once in a while; to afford an iPhone, to call Fido, as Qadir Bhai did, and give his full name and address and date of birth and make a *complaint*, or *demand* a better deal.

Someday, he thought. Someday.

His breathing had calmed down a bit. He thought of that home in Abbotsford again. How astonishing it would be to actually own something like it. It had a large wooden door with the number 123 on it. Outside, he had a lawn, and a tree that was full in summer and went bald in winter. His breathing slowed down even more. He walked up the three steps to the front door.

But that was all.

Even in his dreams, he did not have the guts to enter his fake home.

The next morning, Abdul sprang out of bed. The grayness of the night before was almost gone, and the rays of the sun came in through his small window, a reminder that perhaps there was gentleness in store for him after all. He pressed the power button on his old Nokia cell phone — it took forever to come on — and saw that he had a text message from Randy. He would get a ride from Surrey to North Vancouver where his cricket club was. He quickly gobbled down two boiled eggs and waited for Randy to show up.

Randy was a South Indian businessman, who had started out as a restaurateur. He was built like a wrestler — short, stocky, hard as hell, and he opened the batting with Abdul. Due to his muscular physique, he couldn't run fast between the wickets, but when he hit the ball, he hit it out of the ground, so there was no need to run. Together, the two of them had had some outstanding partnerships and had garnered the North Van Cricket Club some serious acclaim.

"Mr. Abdul," said Randy. "Long time!"

Randy always called Abdul by a myriad of names. It was Mr. Abdul, Abdul Bhai, Abdul the Great, Abdullah, but never Abdul. Abdul never bothered to ask him why. There was a cadence in Randy's voice and Abdul felt feted when Randy called his name, donned with some grace that he would never get from real life.

"How are you, man?" Randy asked.

"Me good," said Abdul.

"*I'm* good, man. *I'm* good!"

Randy also took it upon himself to be Abdul's English teacher. Randy's English was impeccable — in fact he spoke it better than most Canadian-borns, each word so clear Abdul felt that English acquired some serious biceps under Randy's tongue.

"*I'm* good," said Abdul. He wished Randy could have tutored him in English all throughout the year, but it was only for a few months, four to be precise, that Randy was a part of Abdul's life. Come September, once cricket season was over, his teammates went back to their lives and he to his.

It felt so strange, so exhilaratingly strange, to sit in a car.

Randy had a Lexus GX 470, an SUV, and it made the other cars look tiny, as though Randy was seated on a throne that moved stealthily, a silent turbo-powered crocodile, unlike Qadir Bhai's van, an old, decrepit vehicle that smelled of vegetables and goat and had grains of rice strewn on the mat. Qadir Bhai had an expensive car too, an Audi, but Abdul never sat in that. That was reserved for Qadir Bhai's family. "You are like a son to me," Qadir Bhai had once told Abdul in that same liar voice that he used for the immigration folk. But that son never got to sit in the Audi.

"Come on, for fuck's sake," muttered Randy.

The car ahead was doing a 100kph, but that wasn't enough for Randy. He could go faster, wanted to go faster, and Abdul understood. A hundred wasn't enough for Abdul either — on the cricket field. While very few batsmen could even dream of scoring a hundred runs in the league that Abdul played in, Abdul was always hungry for more.

"You know, Al Pacino has this same car," said Randy.

"Oh."

"You do know who Pacino is, right?"

"Scarface," said Abdul.

"Right on," said Randy.

Randy put some music on — it was techno, and it made Abdul feel like they were in space. They sped through the highway that led to North Van, and Abdul never failed to marvel at the stretch of tall trees that lined either side of the road. The air was so crisp here, and he immediately thought of India's highways, long dusty stretches of death, where transport trucks bullied every other vehicle, and accidents were so common they were cleared up like the day's garbage.

"So … how's things at the restaurant?" asked Randy.

"Fine, fine … all good."

"Any new specialties from Master Abdul?"

"Nothing new," said Abdul. "Same mutton, same chicken."

"As long as it tastes good, right?"

"Right…"

Randy suddenly lowered the volume. The techno still played but it was faint; it seemed to come from very far away.

"Listen, Abdul, I want to talk to you about something."

It was the first time Randy had called him by his name.

"I'm opening an Indian restaurant downtown. And I'm wondering if you'd like to come work for me," said Randy. "What's your PR status like? Did it come through??

"Nothing come through…" said Abdul.

"But have you applied for it?"

"I don't know…"

That was the whole issue. He had no idea what was going on. All he knew was that his passport was sitting in Qadir Bhai's home, and each time Abdul asked Qadir Bhai what was going on, Qadir Bhai would say, "Abdul, my son, immigration laws have changed." Then he was told how complex the laws were, how nuanced, as Qadir Bhai twisted his hands this way and that, which reminded Abdul of the way serpents moved.

"If you come work for me, my lawyer will handle things," said Randy. "I'll make sure you're able to work in my restaurant as a chef. Legally. I'll pay you well and you'll get your Canadian residency, no strings attached. You can walk out of my place the day you get it."

Abdul was taken aback. Randy had eaten at the Moon a few times, and had mentioned how much he liked the food, but this was a surprise. Randy had an array of chefs who worked for him. Abdul was a cook. But now Randy had called him a "chef."

Rodrigo Valenzuela, *Barricade No. 1*, 2017, archival pigment print mounted on Sintra, 55.5 by 45.25 inches (framed) / Courtesy the artist and Klowden Mann Gallery

"Are you gonna say something or what?"

Abdul realized he had gone totally silent.

"But Qadir Bhai … he…"

"Let me take care of Qadir Bhai," said Randy. "All I need is a yes from you."

"I…"

"Take the rest of the week to think it over. But I'll need an answer by next Sunday."

Abdul nodded. This had come out of nowhere, a total googly.

If Qadir Bhai even got a whiff of this conversation, he would fly into a rage. What if he just threw Abdul out? What if he destroyed Abdul's passport? Qadir Bhai was the kind of man who demanded loyalty. If it weren't for Qadir Bhai, Abdul's brother wouldn't be able to attend school in Bombay. Hasan's fees were taken care of, his books were taken care of, his uniform, everything. In a year, Hasan would give his 10th-grade finals and then be ready for college. Abdul did not want to jeopardize that. That was one promise Qadir Bhai had kept. Five years ago, when he had visited the slaughterhouse in Bombay and had spoken to Abdul's employer, Ali Bhai — his friend from the old days — he'd placed his hand on the Qur'an and said, "I will make Abdul a Canadian citizen. But it will take time." It had taken too much time, Abdul knew, but the other promise had been kept, in its entirety.

Randy took the turn toward Norgate Park, past the Iranian grocery store where a woman was stacking up watermelons. Randy parked the car just behind the clubhouse and took his cricket gear out of the trunk. Abdul only had his bat with him, and a ball guard — you couldn't share those — everything else he borrowed from his teammates, and they were more than happy to lend him whatever he wanted because he was their ace. The team even chipped in and paid his club fees.

If only his brother could see how beautiful the ground was.

Abdul took the air deep into his lungs. It tasted great. How much better it would taste, he thought, when it was finally his.

He scanned the ground and remembered all the places he had hit the ball last season: he almost hit the totem pole, but was glad he didn't. The Indian reservation was just behind the ground, and he didn't want to offend anyone. Then he looked at the trees in the distance where balls had left dents in the trunks. Then something caught his eye. Something that wasn't there before. He could hardly believe it. Through the trees, he saw the white marbled minaret of a mosque. A year ago, it used to be a church.

"When they build?" he asked Randy.

"Build what?"

"That," he said, pointing to the mosque.

"Oh. They started after the cricket season was over. Came up pretty quick, didn't it?"

Like magic, thought Abdul. Suddenly, he felt elated.

There were other mosques in the city, but he'd never felt like going to any of them. He missed his mosque in Dongri — it was the only one he ever went to — the same mosque where his father had taught him how to pray. The very first time he had gone, when he saw the way his father closed his eyes, he felt a calm come over him, as though his father, by closing his eyes to this world, was opening them up to another. Then, years later, it was Abdul who held Hasan's hand and took him on his first visit to the mosque. Two boys without parents, kneeling together, who knew all they had was each other. When Hasan asked Abdul why they had to pray, Abdul replied, "To give thanks to Allah."

"But Allah took Abba and Ammi-jaan away," said Hasan.

"But He left me for you," said Abdul. "And you for me. So we give thanks."

Then, at night, the singers would come on. They would send their voices into the air, proof of their love and longing for the divine. Each time they sang "Dongri *ke* Sultan," Abdul was convinced that song was prayer too. The words, the kneeling, they were just the beginning. The songs went into the air, they circled around the minarets, rested on the domes, and then continued upward, toward Allah, and at night showed themselves to the faithful in the form of stars.

Perhaps the appearance of this mosque in North Vancouver was a star, and the fact that it was right next to the cricket field made it shine all the more brighter. Maybe all that begging and kneeling at the back of the restaurant had reached Allah, and Allah had sent a sign. It had been here all along, waiting for Abdul.

Just like Randy's job offer.

Qadir Bhai, a man who shared the same faith as Abdul, had let him down.

And here was Randy, a South Indian — a Hindu — lending a helping hand, offering to make him visible. That made Randy more Muslim than Qadir Bhai.
Only one who behaved truly was a true Muslim. One who kept his promise. Why should Abdul be loyal to someone who had betrayed him? Someone who had used his passport as leverage? Who made promises in India and pretended that they did not count in Canada.

Qadir Bhai had another restaurant in Calgary, another Mughlai Moon, and when Abdul had asked him who worked there, he always evaded the question, until it slipped out of his son's mouth one night, when he had woken Abdul up and demanded some dinner for him and his drunken friends. There was another "Abdul-type" in Calgary, Qadir Bhai's son had said to his buddies, another Bombay boy. Was he hiding at the back of the moon as well? Was this how Qadir Bhai bought his Audi?

Abdul looked at the cricket field. The grass was green, the color of Islam. Another sign, another show of strength. He bent down and felt it against his palm. One afternoon, on a chance visit to Stanley Park, Abdul had discovered that cricket was played in Canada. The soft carpet of grass was a revelation to him. Unlike the dusty *maidaans* of Bombay which sent him home with cuts and bruises, the grass was a homely rug — gentle and inviting. He had literally gone to sleep on it, felt it against his back. After being in Vancouver for over a year, it was the first time he had smiled. And the grass smiled too. People never smiled at him, but the grass smiled.

Now, as Abdul looked at Randy, the people were smiling too.

By the time Abdul got out to bat, the clubhouse was packed. The first game of the season always brought the immigrants and their families out of hibernation, and they drank beer and cooked burgers and smoked cigarettes while Abdul hammered the bowlers around.

Abdul always played under a fake name. Ever since the British Columbia Mainland League started uploading the scores on line, Abdul did not want to take a chance. Not that the immigration authorities had the time to monitor cricket websites, but you never knew. Today he was Manny, short for Manpreet. Manny was still out on a mining contract in Calgary, and when Manny returned, Abdul would use another player's name. But over the years, the opposition knew and they didn't care — it was an unspoken rule that immigrants would never tell on another immigrant. They understood each other's pain all too well.

Abdul and Randy were batting effortlessly. Both the opening bowlers, no matter how fast, had been ineffective.

"We make good partners," said Randy. "See?"

There was no doubt about it. They were creaming the bowlers, and the captain of the bowling side was getting very frustrated. He kept making comments about how Randy only had one shot to offer, a cross-batted swing, and that if it weren't for Randy's age, they'd bowl much faster — they said anything to piss Randy off. Abdul could see that Randy was turning red and would burst any second.

"Hey, Randy," their captain said. "How come you're so fat?"

"Because each time I bang your wife, she feeds me a biscuit," Randy replied.

Suddenly, all hell broke loose. The captain started abusing Randy, and Randy refused to back down. The umpires had to intervene. The opposition's captain had resorted to sledging to throw Randy off balance, but it had backfired on him.

"That prick," said Randy.

"No worry," said Abdul. "I show him."

Sure enough, the next over, the captain decided to bowl, to try his hand at getting Randy and Abdul out.

"I'll tell you what," said Randy. "If you hit this guy out of the ground, I'll give you a raise."

"I don't know my salary even," laughed Abdul. "So how I know if raise?"

"Just humiliate him. Make him long for his mummy."

"I do for you, man," said Abdul. After all, this could be his future boss. If someone insulted Qadir Bhai, Abdul would have done the same.

Just before Abdul faced the next ball, he looked at the mosque, closed his eyes, and said a quick prayer. When the red cricket ball came at him, he saw it like it was a football. He stepped out of his crease and lofted the ball high into the air. It just seemed to take off into the stratosphere. It looked like it was going to clear the net that had been placed across the end of the ground — the city had received complaints that the cricket ball was landing on the roofs of the homes that lined one end of the ground, so the club had now put up a net, 50 feet high, across that side of the field, to prevent the ball from going there.

But not this ball.

No one had cleared the net before, and every single player on the field followed that ball as it soared over the net. Abdul's smile quickly vanished when he heard someone scream. It was an elderly woman working in the garden of one of the homes.

"Shit!" said Abdul.

He bolted across the field toward that home. Randy followed. It took them a couple of minutes to get to the garden because they had to go around the netting. The woman was holding the ball in her hand. Abdul was relieved to see that she wasn't hurt. But she was angry.

"What is wrong with you people?" she screamed.

"I ... I so sorry..." said Abdul.

"This could have killed me!" she said. She was pressing the ball in an effort to demonstrate how rock hard it was, but she didn't need to. Abdul knew.

She wasn't angry. She was terrified. If that ball had hit her head, it would have been the end for her. She was almost shaking, and Abdul realized that some of the players from the fielding team had gathered behind him as well, just to make sure that she was okay. But it wasn't helping. The woman was getting more and more uncomfortable. Abdul saw what she was seeing — all these men, bald men, hairy men, men with goatees and spiky hair descending upon her garden, casting a shadow on her flowers, and the fact that they were all brown and she was white wasn't helping either

Abdul turned to Randy and the others.

"She scared..." he said. "You go, please ... I speak."

"We need that ball," whispered the captain. "Make sure you get the ball back."

"This is too much!" she shouted. "Every goddamn summer!"

"I ... my mistake..." he said. She was panting now, and he was too — he had run all the way to her; he too was pumped up with fear.

Just as he was about to apologize further, the front door opened and a boy of about 14 stood before him. Abdul was relieved. It would be more appropriate to apologize to the boy. He was too conscious of the fact that it was an elderly woman he had scared — that too, someone white.

"Buddy," he said as he walked toward the boy. "I so sorry, I hit ball in garden..."

"Don't go near him," said the woman.

"Is okay..." said Abdul. "I just say sorry."

As soon as he was a couple of feet away from the boy, the boy started screaming. He started hitting his head against the front door. Abdul had no idea what was going on. He also felt extremely aware of his cricket gear — here he was wearing cricket pads and gloves, and he had a bat in his hand. Was the bat scaring the kid? He started retracing his steps. The woman had moved toward the boy and was trying to calm him down. Abdul decided it was best to walk away.

By the time he got back onto the field, some of the players were sleeping on the grass. They seemed unperturbed by what had just happened. Perhaps nothing had happened, Abdul told himself. But if nothing had happened, why were his nerves so jangled up? All the cricket gear that he was wearing suddenly felt so heavy. He needed a glass of water, some sugar perhaps.

"Did you get the ball?" asked Randy.

He had forgotten the ball. Or maybe he hadn't. Maybe the ball was the one thing he was thinking of: it landing on the woman's head, cracking her skull, her lying there on the soft green grass, on a bed of yellow flowers and dark red blood. He was feeling dizzy, and the sun was beating down on him. As he walked toward the clubhouse, the smoke from the barbecue grill entered his nostrils.

"Great shot, Abdul," said someone. "That was a monster six!"

He shook his head, and wondered if they could see that his hands were shaking too.

The next day, Abdul was woken up from his sleep by a loud banging on the door. He had been dreaming about the boy. He thought it was the boy who was banging his head on the door. But it was Qadir Bhai. Abdul had overslept.

Without eating any breakfast, Abdul got to work. To appease Qadir Bhai, he cooked him a new dish, something he had promised himself he would never cook for Qadir Bhai because it was what his father used to make for him. But he wanted to start his week with something lovely, something kind, so he made egg *bhurji* with mutton in it. Qadir Bhai loved the concoction and asked Abdul to serve it in the restaurant the very next day.

Instead of allowing Abdul to bask in the glory of this new offering, Qadir Bhai accepted all the compliments of the customers with a gracious nod as though he had been finessing the *bhurji* for months and had finally perfected it. Abdul saw Qadir Bhai's bloated ego, his good mood, and decided to ask.

"Qadir Bhai," he said. "Just wondering if there is any news on my visa."

"*Beta*," Qadir Bhai replied. "You know how it is..." Then he lowered his head and spoke softly in Hindi, always softly when delivering bad news, lies, always softly. "You'll have to wait for a few more months."

"But it's been so long," said Abdul. "Five years."

"I know," said Qadir Bhai. "I have to find a new lawyer, you see. My lawyer passed away — he was my friend, a fellow Muslim, who had offered to do this job for free, but his son is not cut from the same cloth. His son wants his full fee. Five thousand dollars."

"Five thousand?"

"What can I say? These young people have no soul..."

Perhaps you are talking about your own son, thought Abdul. How badly he wanted to say it.

"Give me one more year," said Qadir Bhai. "I will sort things out."

"If you give me a loan, I will work my way through it, I swear. Please, Qadir Bhai. I just want to be legal here. I want to go back to Bombay, meet my brother and come back here. As resident of Canada, not as a thief. I feel like a thief. Pay the lawyer and I will work off the debt. Please!"

"Where will I get the money from? The restaurant is not doing well. And whatever money I earn, some of it I send for your brother's education. I pay you as well..."

"You pay me minimum wage," said Abdul. "Sometimes less."

"Abdul, times are tough. Please have faith in Allah. If Allah wills it, it will happen."

Perhaps Allah wants you to sell your Audi. Perhaps Allah wants you to stop giving cash to that worthless son of yours. Perhaps Allah wants you to keep your word.

Abdul did not back down. He just stood there in silence hoping to make Qadir

Bhai even slightly uncomfortable for bringing Allah into this. But Qadir Bhai leaned on Allah even more.

"Allah will find a way," he said.

Yes, thought Abdul. Allah will find a way. Perhaps he already has.

That night, as he lay in bed, the light of his cell phone was the only thing that shone in his tiny room, and it shone with hope, two simple words that gave off fluorescence that could have lit a stadium.

I in, he wrote to Randy.

He stared at the screen for a long time and then pressed "Send."

By the time Sunday came, by the time Abdul and Randy were batting again, Abdul could hardly contain himself. On the way to the ground Randy had called his lawyer, on speaker phone, and the lawyer sounded seasoned, not a bullshit smooth-talker like Qadir Bhai.

"You're batting differently today," said Randy in between overs.

He was right. Abdul was not hitting the ball hard. He was timing it superbly, he had a silken touch, and he wanted to tell Randy it was all thanks to him. He could breathe now, he was more relaxed, and even his hamstrings which were always tight from standing for long hours at work, weren't as taut. They were like the strings of a musical instrument. If you ran your fingers along them, sweetness would be heard.

The bowler was about to come in and bowl a fast one at Abdul when he stopped half way through his run up. He had seen something behind Abdul. When Abdul turned to look behind, he saw two cops walk toward the cricket pitch. One man, one woman. Why were there cops on the cricket field?

When Abdul saw the old lady near the cop car, he knew they were coming for him.

With each step they took, the grass became silent.

"Excuse me," said the male cop to Abdul. "Are you the gentleman who hit the ball into that lady's garden?"

Abdul wanted to say something — a simple "yes" would do but there was a lump in his throat. Nothing came out.

Randy came to his rescue. "Yes, officer," he said. "It was a mistake."

"Please step back," said the woman. She said it from a distance away, and she only held her arm out, but it stopped Randy in his tracks, and it made Abdul go colder.

"I'm asking you," said the male officer to Abdul. "Was it you?"

Abdul nodded.

"What's your name?"

That was the hardest question he had been ever asked in his life. Last week he was Manny. But this week he was Harry, for Harpreet. Manny was back from Calgary. But he wasn't Harry either.

"Sir, I asked you a question," said the cop.

"I ... sorry," said Abdul. "It went by mistake. Over net..."

"I asked you your name."

"My name ... my name Abdul," he said.

"Abdul what? What's your full name?"

"Abdul Siddiqui."

"Did you threaten that lady's grandson?"

"Yes," said Abdul. "I sorry…"

"You *did* threaten him?"

"Officer," said Randy. "He's misunderstood. His English isn't…"

"Please stand back," said the female officer.

"I no say anything," said Abdul. "I only sorry!"

"Calm down," said the officer. "Did you raise your bat toward him?"

"No," said Abdul. "I bat in hand."

"Why did you carry your bat all the way to her home?"

"My bat in hand," he repeated. "My bat in hand!" He tried to calm himself down, but he was sinking.

"That boy had to get stitches in his head," said the cop.

"But *he* bang on door. He crazy!"

"Excuse me?"

"I no mean…"

"Can I have some ID?" asked the cop.

"No ID," said Abdul. "ID home. I play cricket…"

"So you don't have ID? Where do you live?"

He immediately thought of the fake home with the large door, the tree that was full in summer and bald in winter.

"Surrey," he said, and rattled off Qadir's Bhai's home address. What else could he do? A fake address would be the worst thing at this point.

"How long have you been in Canada?" asked the cop.

"One month," said Abdul. The minute he said that, he started smelling.

"Where are you from?"

"Mumbai," said Abdul. "I visiting uncle in Surrey. I go back India next week."

"So you're visiting?"

"Yes," said Abdul. He didn't know what else to say. There were a hundred thoughts running through his mind. He imagined himself being handcuffed and being taken in the back of the cop car. He had seen it in the movies; he had seen it being done in Surrey as well, to some of the very people who ate at the Moon.

"Where do you work?" asked the female officer.

"In restaurant," replied Abdul.

The minute he said that he knew he was gone. He could feel the color drain from his face. He had been tricked. He had made the blunder of his life.

"So you work here?" she asked.

"No, no," he said. "In Mumbai. I cook."

"I see."

"Sir, you'd better come with us," said the male cop. "Just for some questioning."

"But I no do anything," protested Abdul.

"This way," said the male cop. And Abdul knew it was best for him to do as asked. He was a goner the moment the cops stepped onto the field. Who did he think he was

Rodrigo Valenzuela, *Barricade No. 5,* 2017, archival pigment print mounted on Dibond, 55.5 x 45.25 x 2.25 inches (framed) / Courtesy the artist and Klowden Mann Gallery

fooling? No one would come to his rescue. Qadir Bhai would simply deny everything. His hands started shaking.

When Abdul looked at Randy, he could sense the disappointment in Randy as well.

"I being kept here," he said. "I forced to work."

He could not look at Randy. He could feel his own shame dripping down his face onto the grass, making it wet and heavy.

With that, he started walking toward the cop car. He could not see the old woman anywhere. She was a vindictive piece of shit. He had done nothing wrong.

"I need help," he told the male cop. "I want to go back India. Please help."

But the cops were silent. As he got off the grass, he bent down and took his cricket pads off. Then his gloves. But he held on to his bat. A second later, even the bat was of no use. It needed to be shed. He left it on the ground.

Somehow, he wasn't shaking anymore. But he felt a strange chattering in his mouth. His teeth were chattering at enormous speed. He felt himself gnawing at something; it was a strange feeling, but altogether familiar as well. As he sat in the back of the cop car, he felt smaller and smaller, grayer and grayer. His brown skin was turning into gray wool. He felt strong. He felt he could eat through metal, through Qadir Bhai's Audi. Then he felt the taste of hard paper in his mouth. He could feel Qadir Bhai's passport between his teeth, a Canadian delicacy that he was nibbling on, much hotter than the coffee at Tim Hortons, more mouth-watering than any deal Fido could offer. He nibbled at it with great relief, then spoke to the cops who were listening so beautifully, more than any white person had ever listened to him, and he could feel the passport turning into a different shape, the edges tearing, as though the outline of a new country was being formed, a country for traitors like Qadir Bhai, where rats like Abdul were in charge, who ensured that promises made were promises kept, and when dreams were offered to people, a thousand rats would start singing, nibbling, gnawing in warning, and shame would drip down the jowls of men like Qadir Bhai, just like Abdul's shame had wet a country that could have been his.

THE WRONG STUFF

HELEN DEWITT

Back in January the *Guardian* published a Q-and-A with Zadie Smith to mark the publication of a new book of essays. Hans Ulrich Obrist, artistic director of the Serpentine Galleries, asked:

> What is your unrealised project, your dream? We know a great deal about the unrealised projects of architects, but almost nothing about those of artists or writers. Doris Lessing once said that besides the unrealised, there are also those projects that we self-censor, those which we do not dare to do.

I was consumed with envy. I can't do justice to Obrist's career here; suffice it to say that he is a curator who takes Diaghilev as his inspiration. If *only*, if *only*, if *only* he had asked me!

I could have explained that I had a hundred-odd unrealized projects immured on my hard drive, projects of which agents had said No Publisher Will Allow, projects that could change the face of 21st-century fiction. Projects that were not even books, so no agent or editor would know what to do with them. I would need a week to set out materials on tables, tack papers to walls, and talk nonstop. Surely the Diaghilev *de nos jours* would like the idea of jumping on the first plane to Berlin.

I could have explained, that is, things that are comprehensible in the art world but the kiss of death in the world of books.

The literary world does quite like the notion of genius, but it has no place for a Picasso. When my first novel, *The Last Samurai,* was published, I was distraught at the loss of time because so many other books had been derailed. I went to agents with a postcard of Vladimir Horowitz, arms folded, standing in front of his Picasso. The pianist of genius had used the money he earned with his performances to buy a single Picasso, I explained. But Picasso owned every Picasso that ever existed. When he wanted to see what Picasso would do next, he went to his studio to do the next thing he wanted to do. If he had had to stop for a year to chase sales, what should he have done with the money? Buy a Braque?

Smith's agent, Georgia Garrett: If you're not interested in sales and publicity, maybe you don't need an agent.

In the art world it's understood that artists get excited by new techniques, new materials. It's understood that artists get excited by conceptual possibilities. How is it possible for two physically indistinguishable objects to be different works of art? How can one be a work of art and another a mere real thing? It's understood that process is interesting in its own right (Alain Delon loved drawings, because they're the place where the idea comes into the world).

A writer who tries to appropriate these paths to ambitious work will make many people profoundly unhappy. There are acceptable ways to be a literary genius; these are not among them.

I've been obsessed for years with Edward Tufte's pioneering work on information design. I was obsessed with games — chess, poker, bridge, scientific whist, the sabermetric approach to baseball, the transformation of football by Bill Walsh's passing game. I thought Tuftean infoviz could make it possible to show these different ways of seeing action and events in fiction. So I would trundle a little suitcase full of materials to meetings with agents and editors, and the meetings would be converted to drinks, coffee, dinner, lunch, anything that ensured available surfaces were monopolized by food and drink.

A Tuftean approach requires technical support during composition of the book, and publishing protocol enforces the strict separation of writers from the production team. The correct procedure is for the author to submit a finished text that can then be handed over to the team, who must be protected from the pollution of contact with the author at all times. There's no place for the practices of the art world, in which gallerists, curators, dedicated collectors visit the artist's studio, in which it's a mark of engagement to extend the artist's scope by supporting technically challenging projects. The disempowerment of the author seems to arise, in part, from the fact that the publishing world is oriented toward derivatives — in the first instance, copies of an object that is already at one remove from the original, in the second transformations of that object into translations, films, and so on. So agents have co-agents in foreign

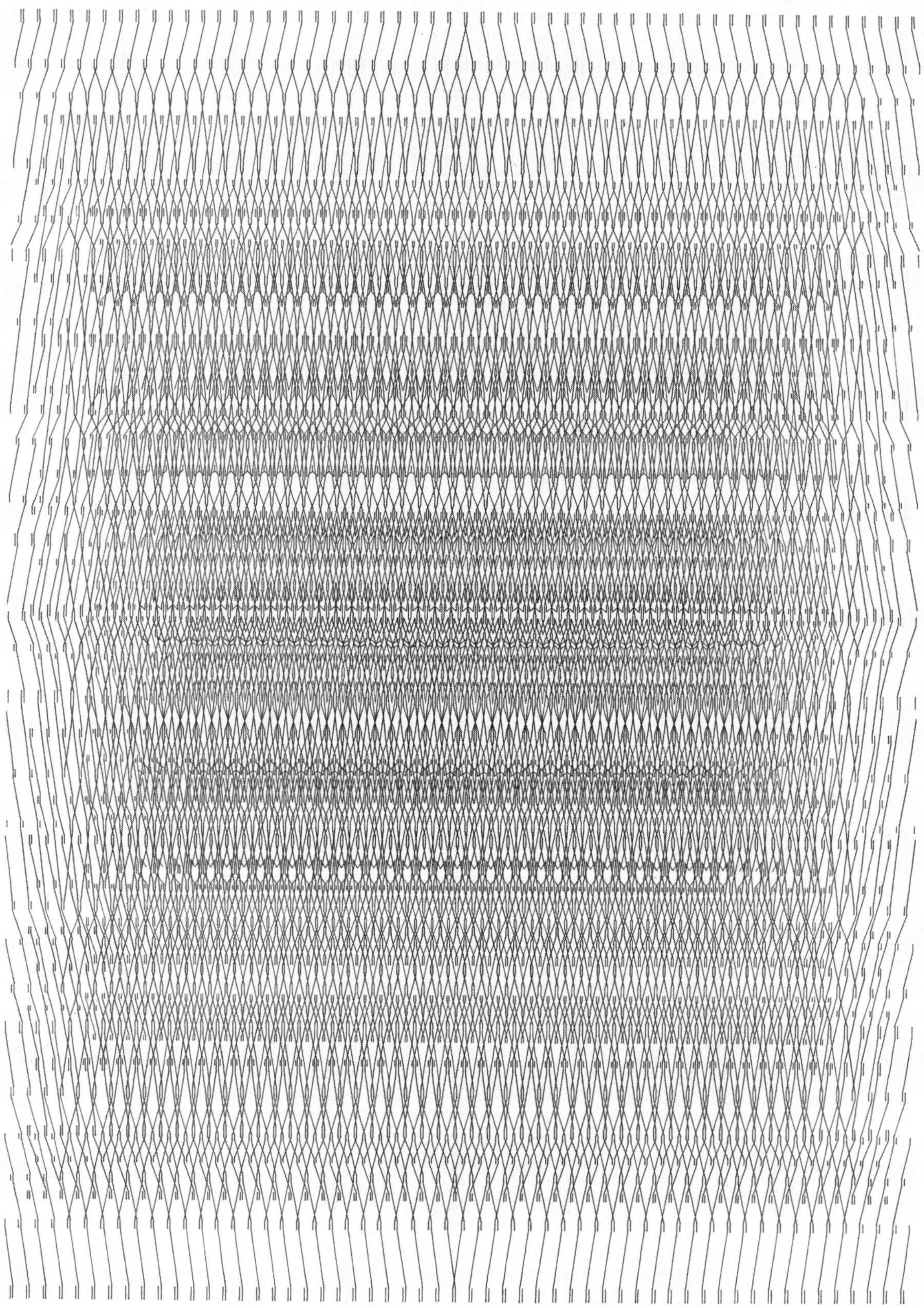

territories, connections in the film business. But there's nothing comparable for connections with the art world, where financial value derives from the premium on originals. So we don't, for instance, see the release of a book coupled with a gallery show with original materials. Perhaps it's not really so interesting to ask how publishing can accommodate a wider range of work; perhaps we need to rethink placing value only in the results of the machinery of legitimacy.

These constraints naturally change a writer's view of her talent. Perhaps you think of something no one has done before, a hundred things that no one has done before, you leap up and down hugging yourself and howling with laughter. You can't naïvely assume you're exceptional. There may be a hundred, a thousand, 10 thousand writers seeing the same possibilities — they will all be told No Publisher Will Allow, they will all be invisible, and so you can't know how many might be jumping up and down at this very moment. If someone, somewhere manages to break through, it will probably be because they got a meeting with the Diaghilev *de nos jours.*

Opposite page: Brian Randolph, *Absorbing Field*, 2017, pen and pencil on paper, 21 x 14.75 inches

SAM'S DREAM

JORIE GRAHAM

One day there is no day because there is no day
before, no yesterday, then a now, & *time*, & a cell
divides and you, you are in time, time is in you, as
multiplying now u slip into our stream, or is it u grow
a piece of stream in us, is it flesh or time you grow,
how, is it an American you grow, week 28, when we
are told dreaming begins. Welcome. Truest stranger.
Perhaps one of the last conceived & carried in womb.
Father and mother singular and known. Born of
human body. Not among the perfected ones yet. No. A

mere human, all first hand knowledge, flying in as if
kindling—*natural*. The last breath before the first
breath is mystery. Then u burn into gaze, thought,
knowledge of oblivion. Rock yourself. Kick so I can
feel you out here. Push your hands against the
chamber. The world is exhausted. I moisten my lips
and try to remember a song. I have to have a song to
sing you from out here.They say you now hear *vividly*.
This could have been a paradise my song begins. No,
this is, was, is, never will be again, will be, we hope

desperately wasn't a dream, maybe in your dream
now there is a clue, can you dream the clue, you who
are dreaming *what* having had no life to dream *of*,
dream *from*—what populates you—bloodflow and
lightswirl, stammering of ventricles, attempts at
motion, absorbings, incompletions, fluidities—do you
have temptation yet, or even the *meanwhile*—such a
mature duration this meanwhile, how it intensifies
this present—or *nevertheless*—no *beyond* of course
in your dream what could be beyond—no

defeat as so far no defeat—cells hum—no *partiality*
as all grows in your first dream which is the dream of
what you are—is that right—no *attempt* as there is
no attempting yet—no *privacy*—I laugh to myself
writing the word—oh look at that word—no
either/or—but yes light filtering-in, root-darknesses,
motion—and the laughter, do you hear it from us out
here, us, can you hear that strain of what we call
sincerity—Oh. Remain unknown. Know no daybreak
ever. Dream of no running from fire, no being shoved

into mass grave others falling over you, dream of no
bot, no capture filter store—no algorithmic memory,
no hope, realism, knowing, no quest-for, selling-of,
accosting violently to have, no lemon-color of the end
of day, no sudden happiness, no *suddenly*. It is much
bigger, faster—try to hear *out*—this place you're
being fired into—*other* in it—*judgment of other*—
logic, representation, nightmare—how to prepare
you—what do you dream—what must I sing—it says
you cry in there & laugh—out here a late October

rain has started down, soon you shall put your small hand out & one of us will say slowly and outloud *rain* and you will say *rain*—but what *is* that on your hand which falling has come round again in the forever of *again* to reach your waiting upturned hand. I look up now. Clouds drift. Evaporation is a thing. That our only system is awry a thing. That u will see rains such as I have never seen a thing. Plain sadness, this hand-knit sweater, old things, maybe u shall have some of—in this my song—in my long song not telling u about the

paradise, abandoning my song of what's no longer possible, that song, it is a thing. Oh *normalcy*, what a song I would sing you. Child u shall god willing come out into the *being known*. First thing will be *the visible*. That's the first step of our dream, the *dream of here*. You will see motes in light. And lights inside the light which *can go out*. A different dark. And spirits, wind exhaustion a heavy thing attached to you—your entity—as u enter history and it—so bright, correct, awake, speaking and crying-out—begins. And all the

rest begins. Amazing, you were not *everything* after all. Out you come into legibility. Difference. *Why shouldn't all be the same thing?* It's a thing, says the stranger nearby, it's a new thing, this stance this skin like spandex closing over you, it's you. A name is given you. Take it. Can you take it? All seems to be so overfull at once. Now here it is proffered again, this sound which is *you*, do u feel the laving of it down all over you, coating you, so transparent you could swear it *is* you, really you, this *Sam*, this crumb of life

which suddenly lengthens the minute as it cleans off
something else, something you didn't know was
there before, and which, in disappearing now, is felt.
The before u. The before. That dream. What was that
dream. There, as if a burning-off of mist, gone where—
not *back*, where would *back* be—dried away—a
sweetness going with it—no?—feel it?—I do—I
almost smell it as it is dissolved into *the prior* by
succession, by events, not raging, not burning, but
going—nothing like the loud blood-rush in the

invisible u & u in with its elasticities, paddlings, nets,
swirls. In this disunion now stretch. Take up space.
You are that place u displace. That falling all round u
is gazing, thinking, attempted love, exhausted love,
everything, or it is everyone, always going and coming
back from some place. They do not stay. *They do not*
stay. And then out here circumference. One day you
glimpse it, the horizon line. You are so...surprised.
How could that be. What are we in or on that it stops
there but does not ever stop. They tell u try to feel it

turn. The sun they will explain to you. The moon.

How far away it all becomes the more you enter. How

thin you are. How much u have to disappear in order

to become. In order to become human. Become Sam.

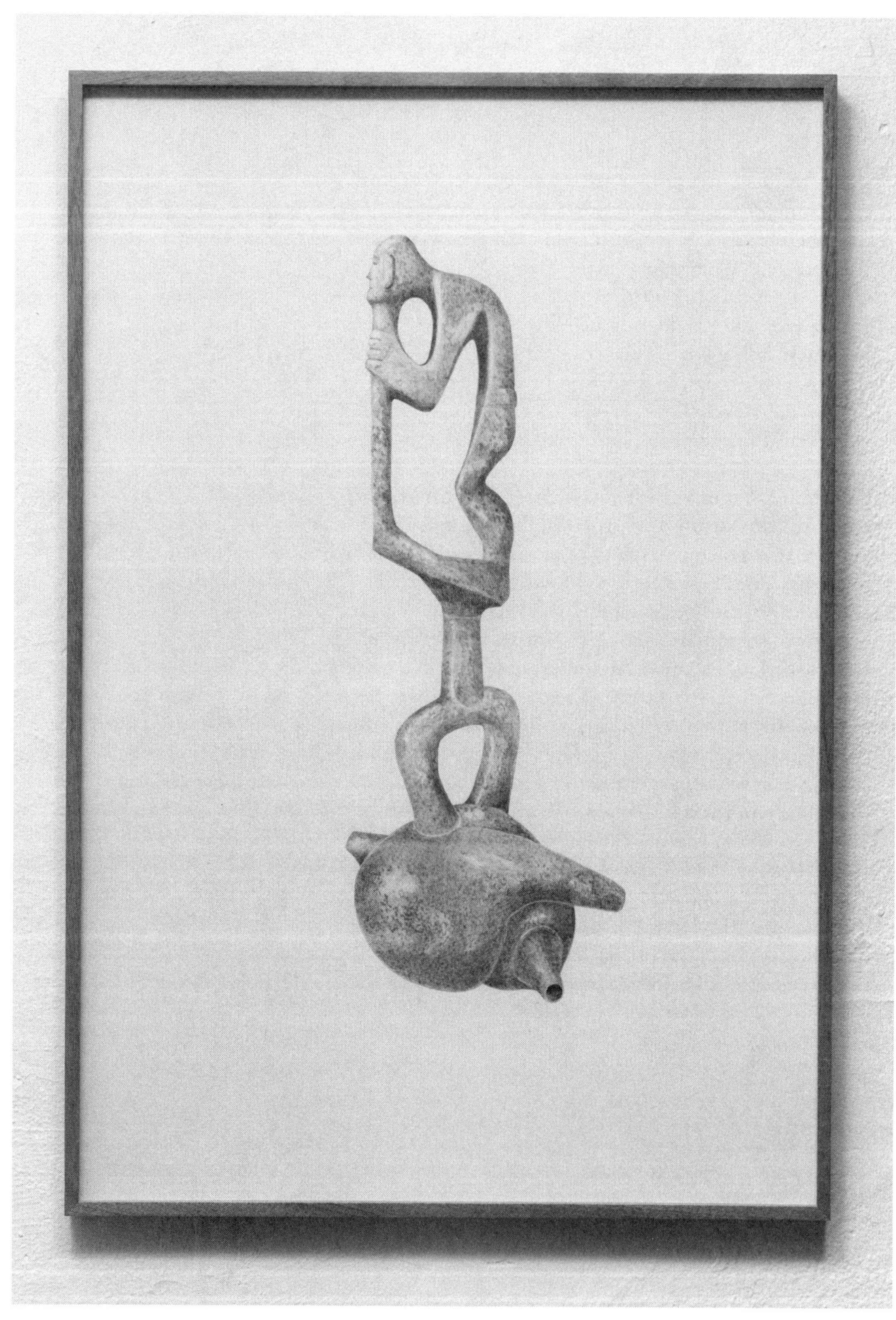

Gala Porras-Kim, *Future spaces replicate earlier spaces (staff/vessel)*, 2017, graphite on paper, artist's frame, 25.75 x 18.75 x 1.5 inches / Courtesy the artist and Commonwealth and Council. Photo: Ruben Diaz

MARTYR AT THE PICNIC TABLE

AARON ROBERTSON

In the Basilica di Santa Margherita, which overlooks the expansive Val di Chiana in Tuscany, Margaret of Cortona's relic is kept in a small casket. The patron saint of the dispossessed, canonized by Pope Benedict XIII in 1728, has been housed inside her glass shrine for centuries. Margaret was not an obvious candidate for sanctitude. She was born in Laviano, Umbria, to a peasant family. At 16, she fled with a nobleman from Montepulciano. Nearly 10 years later, when the nobleman was found mangled in a forest, Margaret moved with her son to Cortona where she led a life of penitence and self-mortification. As proof of her contrition, she asked to be dragged through the streets like an ass by a rope around her neck. Margaret could not tolerate her own beauty. A friar caught her before she could hack off her nose and lips, the iconography of her great allure. In her twilight, she reprimanded vice and experienced many ecstasies before dying in a small cell within the church that would become her temple.

The casket rests on a marble altar, on which scenes from Margaret's life are engraved. The altar is the work of sculptor Gano di Fazio, but the reliquary was designed by Baroque painter and craftsman Pietro da Cortona. St. Margaret has been dead since the 13th century, but her corpse bears no evidence of putrefaction. She is a small woman. All but her head and feet are covered by a sand-colored tunic. The skin on her face is ashen and dry, and it looks as though someone had placed a burlap sack over her head and pulled taut until her eye sockets and mouth were outlined in the cloth. According to Catholic orthodoxy, Margaret is incorrupt. Her corpse was not found to be embalmed, mummified, or dressed with spices. The intact body is supposed to be an expression of divine favor.

The corpse, as a category, is a storehouse for the fantasies of the living. In times of medieval sickness, its organs were thought by some to contain medicinal unctions and oils. In times of war, encomia were written to praise the anonymous dead. The maturation of burial practices signified the presence of civilization, as though the division between brute and man was the degree to which one embellished the dead, cast glory upon them, and escorted them into memory. St. Margaret, though inanimate, is still a prominent actress. She was kept alive by those who couldn't fathom the idea that a body once inhabited by a holy soul could be dismissed as a vessel of dust and earthworms. As historian Thomas Laqueur writes, "The corpse represents something radically different from itself." Whether or not Margaret's soul is immortal, imagination has prolonged her — and others like her — in ways that were not inevitable. The cadaver stiffened by rigor mortis is yet limber in our cultural theater.

Similarities between the treatment of two peculiar types of corpses have been alluded to, but left understated. That is, the bodies of Christian saints and the mutilated remains of African-American martyrs. Our understanding of martyrdom must be fluid. The martyr figure often whets his performative abilities against the stone of persecution. Death may canonize his fugitive sufferings, but alive he can acquire the gaping stigmata and stinging gashes that testify to his capacity to watch the flesh deform. The expressive *sacra rappresentazione* (sacred performance) exhibited by Polycarp or St. Jerome and the brutalization of lynch victims Henry Smith and Jesse Washington are similarly theatrical, notwithstanding some important distinctions between them.

When we talk about the black martyr, do we mean the retributive, self-destructive prophet, like Nat Turner? Maybe we speak of the messiah, like Dr. King, or the unwilling lamb, George Stinney? These models are useful for more than the writing of a martyrology, a *Golden Legend* or *Actes and Monuments* for condemned blacks. The particularities of one's death allow us to better understand both the corpse's appeal as a fetish object and its usefulness as currency. In the schema of black martyrdom, if death is the mytheme — the invariable element that unites all other myths — then the corpse's contours, its stench and solidity, its dissolution and repose determine how and by whom it can be mobilized.

❧

Moribund flesh and viscera have been likened to food in the ways that they are dressed, vitalized, and virtually consumed by the living. Late historian and gastronomist Piero Camporesi identifies body parts as the "tormented protagonists" of the Middle Ages. Holy corpses were tampered with like any well-dressed holiday turkey, prepared as they were with unguents, poultices, and greases. While the souls of saints gloried in the ether, subsisting on light and air, living hedonists occupied themselves with dead chaff.

The sensational account of St. Clare of Montefalco, an Augustinian abbess, is telling. After Clare succumbed to illness, a group of ecstatic nuns opened her corpse with a razor, removed her intestines, and placed them into earthenware jars. The four nuns are said to have marveled at the woman's gallbladder and heart, the latter of which they severed in two. The witnesses claimed that, embedded in the abbess's heart, were the Arma Christi, the instruments associated with Christ's Passion. Among the grisly inventory were a miniature crucifix, the Scourge, the Crown of Thorns, and three nails — a verification of the Trinity's presence. These claims withstood the scrutiny of bishops, theologians, doctors, and civic judges. Camporesi believes this was one of many collective delusions that drifted across the medieval age. More likely, he supposes, the thorned coronet was a bundle of white nerves, the "nails" nothing more than dark tissue.

Following the inquisition, St. Clare's cadaver was drained of blood — the spirit's conduit, what Camporesi calls "the edible substance" — which was then kept in vials where it boiled during times of cataclysm and woe. Chroniclers wrote that the corpse exuded an odor of sanctity. An intoxicating fragrance, maybe of juniper or rosewater, hovered around her and deflected the corruptive heat of summer. The gentle abbess, stuck in time, embodied sprightliness and longevity. Hers was not the only flesh to be adored as health-giving. In some regions of Europe, bone ashes were imbibed in broth and wine while skull fragments were consumed to combat headaches and epilepsy. Leagues of the afflicted collected the liquefied fat of hanged criminals — a ghastly forefather of ibuprofen — in cups and pots. One form of cannibalism persists in the Catholic tradition as the Eucharist. A taste of Christ's transubstantial body and a swig of His blood give rise to a memorial culture in which food is the direct link between death and life.

Few were so dementedly eager to disfigure themselves as the saints. While the modern world built its cranks and muskets, hermits and anchorites embraced guillotines, stakes, arrows, swords, and fasting — anything to ruin the flesh and subordinate their individuality to the symbol of divine mercy they could become. The post-mortem sweetness of the incorruptible's body was a consolation prize from God.

From the other side of a translucent casket stared the envious onlooker. Her inner state reflected the extent of her immersion in the material world. This was the common person, as malodorous as a carrion flower. If her face was daubed with lily-root and saffron tincture, her innards stank like worm-infested feces. Her cadaver's putridity would confirm what was already known about her tainted soul.

But smells were mercurial and ambiguous. Aromatic jasmine collided with the fetor of latrines. The by-products of dysentery and reeking spoil banks mingled with bitter berries. Sundry scents were discombobulating, in flux. Inevitably, smell guided taste. Air became a macrocosm of the kitchen and the courier of wretched stenches. The bodies of martyred saints were minced, pared, cured, and roasted. Consider the apocryphal tale of St. Lawrence, archdeacon of the early Church, who lived during the age of Christian persecution. When the Roman prefect demanded that Lawrence cede the Vatican's wealth to the empire, Lawrence responded by presenting a horde of the poor and diseased. Though he was likely beheaded, legend has it that he was placed on a gridiron and cooked alive. When one of his sides was sufficiently burnt, he is said to have asked his executioners to turn him over.

Accounts of the renowned martyrdom of Polycarp, Bishop of Smyrna, presaged the descriptions of black lynchings that would fill 20th-century newspapers and postcards. In the year 155 AD, at the order of Irenarch Herod, soldiers arrested Polycarp and brought him to an arena. He rode into the city on the back of a donkey. When he refused to renounce his Savior, we are told that the crowd prepared his pyre with "timber and faggots." A fire was lit and then:

> The fire, making the appearance of a vault, like the sail of a vessel filled by the wind, made a wall round about the body of the martyr; and it was there in the midst, not like flesh burning, but like [a loaf in the oven or like] gold and silver refined in a furnace. For we perceived such a fragrant smell, as if it were the wafted odor of frankincense or some other precious spice.

When the flames failed to kill the bishop, an executioner stabbed him to death. His blood flowed so profusely that it snuffed the fire. Officials wanted to keep the body away from the public because they feared it would be hailed as an imitation of Christ. And so it was. His martyrdom was one that "all desire[d] to imitate, seeing that it was after the pattern of the Gospel of Christ." The saint's corpse proselytized. His grisly wounds testified to the Lord's greatness more directly than a zealot. The beautiful death was true.

ꕥ

Henry Smith is an American Negro from Paris, Texas, an outlaw who killed the white baby Myrtle Vance in 1893. Smith's punishment must be as savage as the man. He asks to be shot instead of ceded to a mob of thousands. He is told that he approaches destiny *ad quod damnum*. He will fit into a martyr's mold as though it were a tailored suit. *But,* Sir Thomas Browne asks, *who knows the fate of his bones, or how often he is to be buried? who hath the Oracle of his ashes, or wither they are to be scattered?*

They transport him to a scaffold in a mule cart. Hot irons scorch his feet, his tongue is set aflame, and his eyes are gouged. They bathe Smith with oil. Fire engulfs him like a coat. The tendons in his arms snap like poor bridge cables and he reaches for his eye sockets with crisp stumps. Smith tears away from his post hollering and burning, and when he crawls away, they toss him back. The next day, the *Aurora Daily Express* describes the collection of Smith's remains: "Every scrap of his clothing was sought by relic hunters, and when all was over fragments of his bones were carried away also."

Gala Porras-Kim, *Mesoamerican Negative Space 2,* 2017, plexiglas, graphite, flourescent light
48 x 32.75 x .75 inches / Courtesy the artist and Commonwealth and Council. Photo: Ruben Diaz

Hagiographic texts are babels of undisciplined history and invention. The saint mutates in successive chronicles written by disciples, clergy, and anonymous scribes until the historical personage is fractured. The body of the saint becomes a stage. The corpse is revived in every retelling and dies interminably. The pious listener accepts the necessity of the decapitated head. Her old eyes glisten with desire and the sublime.

ꝏ

When James Baldwin wrote his short story "Going to Meet the Man," he thought of Jesse Washington, a black man from Waco, Texas, accused of assaulting and murdering a white lady in 1916. Many children at the killing ground were on their lunch hour. Baldwin likens this genre of public execution to a Fourth of July picnic. He writes that the "wind blew the smoke from the fire across the clearing" into the protagonist's eyes and nose. The protagonist senses "the odor of something burning which was both sweet and rotten." What do they taste, these children, women, and men? Before castrating the lynch victim, a man weighs the accused's scrotum in his hand like a meat merchant. When they finish, the deceased's head is blackened pulp. At the story's closing, the protagonist tells his son, "I reckon we better get over there and get some of that food before it's all gone." In truth, attendees stole Washington's bones, genitalia, and teeth. Some were sold, others kept. Like triumphant Achilles, the denizens watched as this Hector was dragged through the town by horses.

With the help of civil rights activist Elisabeth Freeman, W. E. B. DuBois and the NAACP used the photographs of Waco resident Fred Gildersleeve to promote their anti-lynching campaign. News of the "Waco horror" resounded in nooks and dailies from America to Europe. The lynching, the most notable of its day, was condemned by most. Lynching had not reached its apotheosis, but the publication of Washington's mutilated corpse tempered rhetoric in support of the practice. The specificity of the violence — Washington's body, and no one else's — was made general. His mourners were not his own. They were rather like paid eulogists, grieving for whomever required commemoration.

These bodies, scoured by crows and all but stuffed into the maws of mobs, glimmered in their chaos. They were unintelligible, unnaturally oriented, decontextualized. Brutalized bodies were denied the grave, and those that were disfigured into anonymity were more likely to be upheld as martyr symbols.

Franny Nudelman, a historian, criticizes the abstraction of pain in her book *John Brown's Body*. The faceless martyr sustains a community based on pain. The unrecognizable corpse was — and still is — an object of great interest because it let empathizers shape something that no longer had an identity. Empathy is possession. The spectator gorges on the suffering of the victim. Nudelman warns against the impulse to glorify and conflate the anonymous dead. It denies the exactness of one's pain and allows the viewer to indulge in limitless orgies of misery.

But imagine the congeries of pilgrims to Mecca and Canterbury. For most, they are palatable in aggregate alone, zooming toward that asymptote where the individual is infinitely indistinguishable from the group. The space between individuals turns into void. We populate it with imaginary emblems. Some of these are born in literature: history books, librettos, novels. Archetypes, in other words, the shadows we cast on the ground.

The black martyr lives. Its ghost threads through Laura Nelson, Denmark Vesey, Addie Mae Collins, Mary Turner, Charles Lang, Michael Griffith, Yvette Smith, Stephon Clark, and Emmett Till. Many little black girls and boys hear Till's story at a young age. I was 10 when I saw the images of that 14-year-old black boy from Chicago who died most horribly in Money, Mississippi, 1955. The story of the inciting incident is as contested as St. Lawrence in flames.

Emmett, with the hesitant approval of his mother Mamie Till-Bradley, is visiting his family Down South. He and some other boys skip church and enter a grocery store, where young proprietress Carolyn Bryant tends to business. Perhaps Emmett whistles at Bryant or says something bold and flirtatious as he exits the store. How little the facts matter. Bryant's husband and brother-in-law abduct Emmett from his uncle's home that evening. He is beaten, shot, and thrown into the Tallahatchie River with a 74-pound cotton-gin fan noosed to his neck by barbed wire. It is a burlesque of the strange fruit swinging from the tree, in the open air.

Emmett plummets into dark waters and, on the third day, is found by two boys gone fishing. After some struggle, his body goes home to Chicago. Two blocks from the funeral parlor, Mamie Till smells a "most terrible odor." When she enters, she doesn't recognize what lies in front of her. Its skin is bloated and its teeth are missing. An eye stretches across the jaw and she can see daylight through its head. Mamie leaves her son's glass-topped casket open for the funeral. Tens of thousands flock to see the child, and images of his body metastasize in black-owned publications across the country. He is the bellwether of aborted democracy. His flesh is rigmarole and confusion. This Christ-figure becomes part of the bedrock that undergirds the nation's Second Reconstruction.

Emmett Till finds new life as a political totem. Mourners blow breath into his battered body in an incredible act of necromancy. Black literati and intelligentsia hallow the boy that had no refuge in an American wasteland. They cradle Emmett in their hosannas and accommodate him in their dreams. The poet Gwendolyn Brooks writes a ballad that fictionalizes Carolyn Bryant. As she awaits the return of her knight-errant, she labors in the kitchen:

> Her bacon burned. She
> Hastened to hide it in the step-on can, and
> Drew more strips from the meat case. The eggs and sour-milk biscuits

Did well. She set out a jar
Of her new quince preserve.

The woman does not know if her life was worth more than that of the "Dark Villain." Her Fine Prince, her husband, beats her in front of their children and she envisages blood. Her blood and the blood of the Villain, who is the innocent child, commingle. The blood is as viscous as fruit spread, a "red ooze" that was "seeping, spreading darkly, thickly, slowly / Over her white shoulders, her own shoulders / And over all of Earth and mars." Emmett's blood terraformed the earth. Its nectar shocked the palate and stirred the insensate masses. They had tasted blood before, white and black alike, but never so publicly. There were thousands of Emmett Tills circulating in private night terrors. The law, for all its pompous austerity, was impotent. After receiving payment for their confession, Emmett's killers walked free. Custom was held as law.

And so Emmett's body was its own advocate and intercessor. Its gnarled limbs pleaded eloquently. Emmett's apostles rendered in speech what the boy had no tongue to say. The interpretation of Emmett's body was unusually cogent: blameless flesh was inconsonant with a culpable, bloody empire.

ꕥ

Sixty years later, the unrest in Ferguson would become a new iteration of an aged myth. The martyr of the Third Reconstruction was born at the instance his body was penetrated by six bullets and Darren Wilson's fretful imagination. Like Mamie Till before her, Michael Brown's mother, Lesley McSpadden, was inducted as the Black Madonna. The Passion of Mike Brown enthralled us because we were uncertain what had led to its lurid conclusion. Eyewitnesses read Brown's body as an archetypal construction. Furious observers noted that the body laid unattended for hours under the sun.

Brown's corpse was the difference between the law as it was and as it should be. It was an expression of insidious, unchanging folkways. Ours is an age of exceptional harvest. Legends are recast and horrific morality tales are authored by gunfire. This juncture is what the postwar historian C. Vann Woodward calls "the twilight zone that lies between living memory and written history." The catalog of executed blacks is Homeric in scope and the boundary between Ralph Ellison's tragic character Tod Clifton and casualties like Laquan McDonald, Amadou Diallo, or Philando Castile is fading, if it has not already dissipated. (Of Clifton, Ellison wrote: "Cause of death (be specific): resisting reality in the form of a .38 caliber revolver in the hands of the arresting officer")

The organizers of Black Lives Matter are storytellers. They architect marches and vigils that evoke the agitations of the 20th century. Their slogans ("I can't breathe") echo and subsume the dead. Their questions ("Is my son next?" "Is my niece safe?"), at once rhetorical and earnest, organize the myth's structure and dictate how it will be told. The questions come from a place of knowledge. They have already been answered and the protesters know this. Their fear is predictive. It is meant to warn. *Yes, my son is next. My niece will be killed. It's his little boy today, her girl tomorrow, and mine is somewhere in line.*

The same basic story retold, with myriad permutations. Its narrators are masterful, always finding some way to make it new. *This one is set in Milwaukee, that one near Detroit. This one was shot at more than 100 times, but that boy only took one.* It is a story the narrators would rather not tell. But they will renew it as often as they must, *ad infinitum* until the body finds its niche in unalienable life, so that its executioner may know the restless charge of firebrands.

Rodrigo Valenzuela, *Barricade No. 6*, 2017, archival pigment print mounted on Dibond, 55.5 x 45.25 x 2.25 inches (framed) / Courtesy the artist and Klowden Mann Gallery

THE PRINCIPAL'S ASHES

JAC JEMC

On the first day of school, the teacher thought only of the first day, not of the 179 school days to follow.

As the students tip-to-tailed in she looked each of them in the eye. Even if they didn't look back, she could see what she needed to see.

Jonah would be the frogbiter, the child capable of taking away a life without an inkling as to what he was doing. The class frog was sure to die before the end of the year because of something Jonah did, not yet realizing that frogs were alive and capable of feeling pain. Mrs. Sayer called this student "the frogbiter" because of the infamous event of 2005, when little Benny Baft had bit off a frog's head in an epic tantrum about having to place his fresh box of crayons into the communal box that all of the children had access to. He'd broken a handful of the wax sticks in half, their soft paper wrappers peeled back as the crayons hit the floor, and then reached into the tank. Mrs. Sayer could have stopped it, but it's true she was tired of cleaning the tank each week. She watched Benny bite the frog's head off and crumple with remorse. She picked up the frog's body with a Kleenex, and sent Benny to Principal Fleer, frog blood running down his chin. She'd get hell from the school nurse for not coming along to explain. Benny was so hysterical, they'd assumed it was his own blood.

Every year this happened, sometimes more brutally than others: bleach in the tank, stapling the frogs hands together, bringing the frog to gym class where he was crushed by a basketball. Every time there was a moment where it was possible for her to step in, but then what? Something else would be the thing to assail the frog, later in the year, and what would the Almighty Frog God say when he didn't get his sacrifice on time? She looked to the event as some sort of harbinger of what the rest of the year held: a groundhog seeing its own shadow. The earlier the frog died, the earlier the trouble began.

The last of the children filed in. Sameera returned her gaze and Mrs. Sayer knew. Sameera would be the one sticking around for a moment after class to ask some philosophical question that Mrs. Sayer didn't have the slightest idea of how to answer, at least to a seven-year-old. These were the interactions she took to her Wednesday wine nights with her friends: *What do you say when the Muslim child asks you if transubstantiation is real after your religion unit? What do you say when she asks you if you ever worry that the kids are smarter than you? What do you say when she says, "I know you're new at this, but…"?* Catholics believe it's real. Every student is smarter than me in some way or another. I've been doing this for 20 years actually.

Mrs. Sayer had been raised Catholic. She taught at the Catholic school because it was closer to her house, not because she still believed and wanted to grow the faith; half the students in the school weren't even Catholic, and it's not as though the ones who were went to church, or believed the pope was infallible, or cared enough to try to attempt converting the others. Mrs. Sayer sometimes wondered why religion, then, was a part of the required curriculum at all. Why not teach religion at the beginning or end of the day, when the students who were interested could stay? Or send the kids who didn't believe to another elective at that time? Religion, in the context of St. Rosa of the Gardens Elementary, was not a class in all of the world's religions: it was catechism. For the 50 percent of the students who weren't Catholic, it was like a course in lying. They could learn the stories like mythology, and the tenets like ethics, but what about all the bullshit that Catholics believed? That, they had to endure, like getting cornered at a cocktail party by your father-in-law who assumes you agree with everything he's saying. She worried about the children who didn't argue or at least screw up their faces with confusion. Maybe they weren't listening. She soothed herself with this thought.

Ellie T's eyes glowed white and centerless. Ellie R kept her face squeezed shut. Danny Zucco (you couldn't make this up) zapped his eyes around without landing assuredly on any one thing. Elizabeth Harvey appeared to be covered in Vaseline. Sam Stockwell moved in a jerky way never seeming to touch the floor. Mrs. Sayer had been in this game long enough to remain unconcerned.

After the students had unpacked their backpacks and organized their cubbies, when everyone was clear on which hook was theirs in the cloakroom, Mrs. Sayer liked to line the students up under the auspices of a bathroom break: girls and boys. On the way, they passed an enamel vase outside the school office, just about as tall as the span of Mrs. Sayer's forearm, elbow to wrist. It sat on a little, perfectly sized shelf. A stack of little knobs, one on top of the other, capped the vase.

"Who can guess what's in here?" Mrs. Sayer asked.

"Brains?" said Jonah.

"In a way."

"Wishes?" said Sameera.

"You're not wrong," Mrs. Sayer responded.

"A dead cat?" said Kim, whose mother, just that morning, had pulled Mrs. Sayer aside and warned her that Kim's cat had just died the week before, and Kim had been morbidly obsessed with it, having dug it up twice already and tried to hide it in her stuffed animal hammock.

"You might be the closest of all," Mrs. Sayer said, smiling. "Inside this vase are the ashes of our former principal, Mr. Fleer. Mr. Fleer is watching us all the time, and it is your job, even when my back is turned, to behave in a way that will make Mr. Fleer proud."

The children fidgeted and focused, fidgeted and focused. Mrs. Sayer didn't ask if they had any questions. She knew well that 19 hands would rocket into the air with unrelated queries. "Let me hear you say, 'Bless us, Mr. Fleer.'" Mrs. Sayer said.

Mr. Allmann passed, wrinkling the wide range between his eyes.

"Wait," Mrs. Sayer said, her eyes on her colleague until he disappeared behind the heavy doors leading to the stairwell. "Okay."

The children shifted their eyes among themselves. "Blefuppmithterflur." It always took a few tries to get the message out clear and concentrated.

As the year progressed, Baldur the frog (only St. Rosa of the Gardens knew where these children learned the things they did) endured, unharmed. Mrs. Sayer answered each of Sameera's questions in such a way that Sameera would smile and nod, temporarily satisfied with her teacher's competence. No scissors cut the palms of hands. No desktops smashed down on fingers. The students abstained from bringing Jell-O cups for their birthday snack after Zaira's presentation on the source of gelatin and so there was no need to make fun of Al, the sole vegan in the classroom. None of the children who knew Santa Claus to be a myth forced their knowledge onto the children who believed. When Mrs. Sayer explained what "waving genitals" were in their poetry unit, no one laughed. It was April, and the class hadn't had to make a visit to Mr. Fleer's ashes to repent.

In the teacher's lounge, Mr. Allmann asked Mrs. Sayer what they were working on that day. Mrs. Sayer sighed.

Every. Single. Goddamned. Day.

"*Howl*," she replied.

"*Howl's Moving Castle* is maybe a little advanced for second graders, no?" he asked.

"Not *Howl's Moving Castle*," she said. "*Howl*, the Allen Ginsberg poem."

"Oh, I'm not familiar," Mr. Allmann responded.

"They love it," Mrs. Sayer said. "After lunch we're going to read the poem aloud together. I pass a jug of juice around and everyone takes a sip. The children shout, 'Go go go!' It takes almost an hour."

"Sounds unruly."

"It is," Mrs. Sayer said. "I lock the doors. At least a couple of the sensitive ones will try to run from the commotion, but that's the lesson. Endurance. Facing the reality of the situation. Finding coping mechanisms."

Mr. Allmann had turned on the faucet to wash his plate, and Mrs. Sayer could tell he either couldn't hear her or had opted not to.

On her way back to the classroom, Mrs. Sayer nodded to the vase on the wall. Mr. Fleer had been a true model of dedication. He had worked at St. Rosa of the Gardens for the entirety of his career, until the day his heart gave out during a spring choral concert, exploded inside of him at the purity and innocence of the children's voices. His will, prepared well in advance as most things he did were, asked that his ashes might "cremain" (Mrs. Sayer couldn't help herself) in the school itself. Technically the Catholic Church demanded that a person's ashes be buried or entombed as corporeal remains must be, but St. Rosa's was progressive, and for someone who had done as much for the parish as Mr. Fleer had, they made an exception.

Mrs. Sayer had always looked up to Mr. Fleer, but she was also determined not to suffer the same fate he had. Most years it wasn't an issue; the children naturally misbehaved from time to time on their own, but this year's class was so composed she saw them as a threat. Her only defense would be to expose them to experience and knowledge beyond their years.

They'd already spent several days breaking down the meaning of the poem line-by-line. Each child had chosen an image from the poem to draw, and Mrs. Sayer had strung them up along the top of the blackboard (St. Rosa's had had a fundraiser so they might update to whiteboards, but they'd not yet been installed).

Evie Sharp had drawn money burning in a wastebasket, William Ferris a man jumping off the Empire State Building, Kayla Kamron drew cigarette burns pocking an arm in a surprising shade of blue. Eagle Crowley painted shoes full of blood, and Ellen Park took on a visual depiction of "mother finally ******." Simeon Paltz chose to turn in a sound recording of his interpretation of a "catatonic piano." Ellery Chin painted that final image of the door to the cottage on a Western night.

She'd read them the section of *Dharma Bums* in which Kerouac described the first night Ginsberg read the poem at Six Gallery. The children bustled, excited for the chance to recreate that infamous night.

Mrs. Sayer was sure the children would get riled. She thought they'd begin to rebel, to tear their books apart, to splash the juice down their shirts, to strike ruler against ruler to spark a fire.

She hoped for nothing less. She wanted to see the children wild out. She wanted cause to understand them as imperfect creatures. She wanted to take them down to visit Mr. Fleer's ashes to apologize for the way they'd behaved. She wanted to arrive at the end-of-the-year ceremony, knowing she would not drown in the deep well of beauty unpolluted inside of them.

Marjana started things off, and the children lolled. They lost interest quickly and Mrs. Sayer yelled at them to pay attention. She pointed to sections of the room, cuing them to shout and clap and holler in support of the words they heard. She'd spent time coaching each of them individually on pronunciation. They'd notated their sections with indications of where to put the emphasis. Some children followed the key more easily than others. Mrs. Sayer let out a whoop of victory when Cristiana Gutierrez finally pronounced "yaketayakking" correctly. She mouthed along "bop kabbalah" with Joe Swearingen, and felt it was to her credit that he finally teased it out without pausing.

She'd assigned the line about "the one eyed shrew that does / nothing but sit on her ass and snip the intellectual golden threads of the craftsman's loom" to Edward Sharma. She could tell he was already well aware of everything in the world that threatened to leave him with nothing.

She knew it would cause waves that she gave the entire Moloch section to Seraphine Bailey, but good god that girl could read at a fifth-grade level, and adrenaline scrambled through Mrs. Sayer. The girl ratcheted up her volume as the second section proceeded, until, unbidden, Seraphine unlatched the window and shouted, "into the street!" right onto the playground where the p.m. kindergarteners looked up in wonder.

Mrs. Sayer saw it as a sign from heaven that the last section of the poem had 19 repetitions of "I'm with you in Rockland," the same number as kids in the class, and each of the children, alert, hovering over their chairs, voiced their part without prompting. The juice sat unfinished, the classroom undestroyed. Mrs. Sayer was proud of their composure, but also disappointed. She *wanted* to visit Mr. Fleer, and so, when the poem wrapped in on itself, she let the silence hold for a moment, deciding what to do.

Outside the principal's office, beneath the urn, Mrs. Sayer told the class, "Mr. Fleer thought you were capable of more, children." She pinged between their faces, still flushed with the exertion of the performance. "Mr. Fleer was counting on you to rebel. Mr. Fleer wanted to see your true nature accelerate out of your soft, stretching bodies, but you failed him today."

ꟸ

At the assembly, on the last day of classes, when parents file up to thank Mrs. Sayer for her service, not one of them will inquire as to why she thought it would be appropriate to teach their children a poem about the way the ethical emergencies of the 1950s caused people's minds to falter. Even Rara's mother won't complain about how her daughter walks around the house repeating a couplet that contains the word "ass." Instead, they will shake her hand and pass her Starbucks gift cards in folded cardboard, bearing the names of their children in a hand too steady to be authentic. When a parent complains about how hot it is in the gym, Mrs. Sayer will stop herself from telling them the world will become uninhabitable before their children's natural lives end. Instead, she will say, "And it's only June," as though the weather were as inexplicable as the Holy Trinity.

Mrs. Sayer will take the last gift card from Jonah, the child she'd identified as the frogbiter, though Baldur still hops around his tank. She will stare into his eyes and wonder how she ever could have thought he was a murderer.

"My favorite Starbucks is chocolate milk," Jonah will say.

When Mrs. Sayer's heart stops, she'll realize she'd been right all along.

GRADUS AD PARNASSUM

RACHEL HADAS

There was a hole in the ceiling
through which I had to climb
if I wanted to get to the next level.
A squarish hole, it looked impossibly small,
but I swung up one leg
and somehow squeezed the rest of my body through
and found myself on the roof of a high building.
On the rooftop: a playground full of children
much too involved in their games
to notice an elderly newcomer
or even to look up.
Having reached the highest level,
I was invisible.

opposite page: Brian Randolph, *Pulse Scroll*, 2018, pen and pencil on paper, 22 x 14 inc

LISA BONET

VENITA BLACKBURN

Okay, so these are the things we have been told never to say in front of children or white people. When I was a kid my grandma used to sprinkle Ajax around the door to keep evil spirits away. It was some voodoo-ramajama-type thing mixed in with Southern Baptist rituals. To this day, I got crazy germ phobias and have trouble kissing my wife. Grandma taught me there are horrors you can't see and can't talk about, but that shit is out there. That was the '90s.

Back then, my wife and I both had a crush on Denise from *The Cosby Show* as kids. There was this episode where Denise sat on Bill Cosby's lap and she was all '80s cool with rainbow cheeks and post-apocalyptic clothes that made her look like a boy who just raided Boy George's closet. She was cool as hell, but even then I thought she looked kinda old to be all on her dad's lap.

I remember when they told us Martin Luther King Jr. was not a perfect man but led a perfect cause. I thought he was bad at math and not bad at fidelity or fatherhood. There were lives at stake so you know, you stay quiet. The books back then made slavery look uncomfortable and irrational, something obviously temporary. They never showed us the tools. The funnels to force-feed slaves who tried to starve themselves to death, the spikes driven into the skulls of infants because blacks were thought to be more likely to survive. Why would anyone have to survive that? It took hundreds of dead babies to prove the theory wrong. My wife told me about the old laws that made it impossible to prosecute the rape of a slave because black women were "lascivious" by nature and, of course, property. Even when I say, "That's terrible," she just looks at me like I don't get it, like no matter how much empathy I can scrape together I'll never know what it's like — the spectacle of female pain when that pain and suffering is ordained by law, performed like theater.

Bill Cosby was always Bill Cosby, but eventually Denise became Lisa Bonet, the actress. She got crazy. Everybody thought she was crazy. They said she and Bill had a falling out. I thought then it was because she wanted to be paid more on the show. Greedy Hollywood bitch, right? So later when Bill Cosby went to court for drugging and raping a bunch of women, we were all…

Today, I want to kiss my wife as often as she'd like, which is too often. She is not strong or proud or wise or witty and is not a perfect best friend. She wakes up too early in the morning, can never find anything, but has good breath. She is not magical, never learned to swim, was severely abused as a child, and is absolutely beautiful like an egg sunny side up. I am not that attractive I'll admit, but she likes how I think and talk and complain, so we're cool.

When she tries to smash her lips on mine, I almost always wince. She tells me I'm traumatized and laughs, but she's hurt, I can tell. It's the bacteria though. I've seen all the documentaries about good bacteria and bad bacteria and how we need some to live and would not survive as a species or planet without them, but in my head they are large as criminals with teeth like a barracuda's all invisible and gnawing away. She looks at me when I try to explain the film on our tongues, and I fail to make it clear. She wants to be patient and not resentful that her childhood looked the way it did and mine didn't, and we are so close to understanding each other but can't quite and are left desperate for some impossible thing. I just want her to close her mouth, so I can love her…

THE NEXT BLACK NATIONAL ANTHEM

JOSHUA BENNETT

Will naturally begin
with a blues note.

Some well-adorned
lovelorn lyric

about how
your baby left

& all you got
in the divorce

was remorse.
& a mortgage.

& a somewhat
morbid, though

mostly metaphorical,
obsession with

the underground.
How it feels to live

in such unrelenting emptiness,
unseen, altogether un-correctable

by the State's endless arms.
Just imagine: Ellison's Prologue

set to the most elaborate
Metro Boomin instrumental

you can fathom, brass
horns & pulsar cannons

firing off in tandem
as Aretha lines a hymn

in the footnotes. Twelve &
a half minutes of unchecked,

bass-laden braggadocio.
The most imitated,

incarcerated human
beings in the history

of the world & every nanosecond
of the band's boundless

song belongs to us.
It is ours, the way

the word *overcome*
or *The Wiz* or Herman

Melville is ours. In any corner
store or court of law, any

barbershop argument
or hours-long spat

over Spades. The Next Black
National Anthem will,

by the rule, begin
in blood, & span

our ongoing war against
oblivion. Clarify the anguish

at the core of our gentleness.
How even that generosity

is a kind of weapon.
This music, our blade

-d criticism of a country
obsessed with owning

everything that shimmers,
or moves with a destination

in mind. Even the sky.
Even the darkness

behind our eyes
when we dream.

TOKEN COMES CLEAN

JOSHUA BENNETT

What I desired most was approachlessness,
enough fear to mark a sharp & ardent

wall between me & the broader social
sphere, think: semi-invisible

force-field, think: aura light
umber like Bruce Leroy.

A beauty one might use to keep
a state-sanctioned grave

at bay, the distance
this darker body ought

to buy but doesn't.
If evolution were kind,

we would all be fireproof
by now. A shame, to be sure: this

brutal truth boomeranging back
& forth across America's oeuvre,

History stammering with blood
in its throat, blood on the books, blood

on the leaves & what can you right
-fully call living now that the dead

have learned to dance so well?
Knife wounds in the global sky,

White god on my childhood mind
& you want to talk about *repair*

Luchita Hurtado, Untitled, c. 1976, charcoal on paper, three parts, each: 14 × 10 5/8 inches
Courtesy the artist and Paul Soto/Park View Los Angeles and Brussels. Photo: Jeff Mclane

NEWS FROM HOME

SARA JAFFE

Recently, my mother read a story I wrote and called me in Portland to ask why she wasn't in it. "It's fiction," I said. The story, which centered on the narrator's ambivalence about having left the East Coast for the West, never mentioned the narrator's mother or any mother or parent. "That's not what the story was about," I said.

Mothers, mine or fictional versions, rarely show up in my writing — unlike the work of Brussels-born filmmaker Chantal Akerman, whose films almost always swarm around a mother's presence or absence. Or both, as in her documentary *News from Home*. The film is comprised of long, fixed takes of New York City street scenes, accompanied by Akerman's voice reading, in French, letters her mother has written her from Belgium. We learn from the letters that Akerman often goes for weeks without sending word, and that the news she sends home is generic, undetailed — she has "a job," "an apartment," "friends" — though it is also possible that Akerman's letters contain details that are inscrutable to her mother, a job or apartment or the kinds of friends her mother would find unimaginable, choices she could not imagine having the opportunity to make or not make.

I think of Akerman's mother as being more present in the film than Akerman herself, but maybe I'm getting it wrong. Though the words are her mother's, it's Akerman's voice reading those words "over" the images, and it's Akerman's hand (literally or figuratively) holding the camera, controlling what we see. Maybe, in figuring Akerman as the absent one, I'm catching her mother's fever. The daughter is in New York, she writes rarely, but how "gone" is she, really? Delusions of loss often precede actual loss. When I first started watching the DVD of *News from Home*, I experienced another kind of absence. The film started, and there was no sound. There were English subtitles, and I found it interesting that Akerman had chosen to subtitle a silent film. Then I got up to check the cords and discovered that the RCA cables were in the wrong holes. I had been willing to accept the film as silent, but as soon as I got the audio straightened out the film's tension materialized. The sound of Akerman's voice reading her mother's letters gave the story shape, brought it into relief.

I also felt relief. I would have watched a silent film, but images don't really absorb me on their own, or I find it difficult to absorb them. I need another sense to activate my engagement — sound, or memory. I was born in New York City in 1977, the same year *News from Home* was released, though the "principal photography" was completed the previous year. Even if I was able to remember the New York Akerman commits to film, I don't think I'd remember it in the way she presents it. The camera stays fixed on the front of a building for three, five, eight minutes; it holds a shot on the subway as the car stops and starts and passengers board, sit, get off. Because the windows are dark there is little sense of movement. Is the long take an antithetical mode in which to render a city where no one stays still for that long? Or are those who stay still — who look out windows, who are sick, who sit on crates — invisible? The long takes prevent me from forgetting that what I am watching is framed, filmed — my distractible gaze would move more often than the camera does — yet in its stillness the camera *feels* absent as it replicates the gaze of the invisible.

My darling girl. Please write more often. We hope everything works out the way you want. Did you get the package, the money, the summer shoes? I don't want to be a selfish mother. Who would? The mother admits she'll never say "Come home." She believes that saying, "Your absence is rending my life apart," is not the same as saying, "Come home." Did Akerman wish her mother would have said "Come home"? Would that have made it easier to get angry, to give definition or purpose to her abandonment?

The film's subtitles add another visual element — a disruptive one? If I knew French well enough to turn them off, I'd get even more mired in the frame. No, "mired" is not quite right — not because I think Akerman would mind me feeling trapped, but because "mired" implies depth. Staying in the frame so long provides not depth but an ever-extending surface. It won't pull me in; *I* need to choose to commit. My boredom attempts to peel back the present, but where can I trust it to take me? (Walter Benjamin: "Boredom is the dream bird that hatches the egg of experience.") "Nothing" happens and then words appear on the screen, a voice starts talking: *My darling girl …*

In one of the film's crowded street or subway scenes, there must have been a woman two, three months pregnant. In late 1976 she would hardly have been showing. Would my mother have noticed the nearly invisible camera? Would I have recognized her? Would she have been thinking about what kind of daughter I was going to be? Akerman, if she had made my pregnant mother the focal point of her film, would not have addressed this question, would not have encouraged the viewer to speculate about my mother's emotional state as she made her way through the city contemplating my imminent birth (was she anxious, dreamy, prematurely heartbroken?). In her narrative work, Akerman does not dig for emotion or examine motivations. "Why?" is the wrong question to ask of a film by Akerman. As in the stories of Jane Bowles, characters in Akerman's films discard sociality for pure id, or a superego so hyperbolic it becomes unmediated, id-like.

But *News from Home* is not a narrative film, it is documentary and collage and epistolary homesick fever dream. The visuals and spoken text neither complement, nor compete with, nor explain each other. They are two surfaces that layer but don't adhere. In the moments immediately after a letter concludes, its absence is palpable, the ear keeps listening for the next one. I try to cohere to the visual field. I look for detail, for movement or change, then I get bored and I want another letter, though I know it's essentially a dead letter and the solace of response will never come.

Around an hour into the film, the frame starts moving, or being moved — we are in a car or bus, driving north up 10th Avenue. The vehicle passes the Port Authority (my adolescent entry point to the city after my parents had moved to the suburbs, one of my mother's great disappointments). I thought that the crescendo implied by the camera's motion meant that the film was nearing its end, but there was another half hour to go. In the real final shot, we're out on the water. On what I imagine is a small raft but must be something bigger. Maybe a ferry. From that vantage the city looks small, gray, ugly, muted. Becomes the postcard she sends that can't reveal anything. Becomes silhouette. We're slowly floating farther from the island.

Luchita Hurtado, Untitled, c. 1970s, graphite on paper, 11 3/8 × 20 5/8 inches
Courtesy the artist and Paul Soto/Park View Los Angeles and Brussels. Photo: Jeff Mclane

UNA GOCCIA

DINO BUZZATI

translated from the Italian by Zoë Slutzky

A drop of water is climbing the steps of the staircase. Do you hear it? Stretched out in bed in the dark, I listen to its arcane journey. How does it do it? Does it jump? Tick, tick, you can hear it on and off. Then the drop stops, and perhaps for the rest of the night it doesn't show up. Still it climbs. Step by step it goes up, unlike other drops that fall vertically, in compliance with the law of gravity, and at the end make a little clack that is well known throughout the world. This one, no: slowly but surely it rises along stairwell E of the endless housing block.

We — adult, refined, highly sensitive — weren't the ones to point it out. It was a servant girl from the first floor, a grimy ignorant little creature. She noticed late one evening, when everyone had already gone to sleep. After a while, she could no longer hold back; she got out of bed and ran to wake her mistress. "Signora," she whispered, "signora!" "What is it?" said her mistress, shaking herself awake. "What happened?" "There's a drop, signora, a drop going up the stairs!" "What?" asked the other woman, dumbfounded. "A drop going up the stairs!" the girl repeated, and almost started to cry. "Go away," cursed her mistress, "are you crazy? Go back to bed, get going! You've been drinking, that's what this is, shameful girl. For a while now wine's been missing from the bottle in the morning! You ugly, dirty thing, if you think..." But the little girl had fled and was already hidden under the covers.

"Who knows what possessed that stupid girl," thought her mistress in silence, by now no longer sleepy. And listening against her will to the night that ruled over the world, she too heard the curious noise. A drop was climbing the stairs, undeniably.

Jealous of its regularity, the lady thought for a second about going out to see. But what could she possibly have found in the miserable light of the clouded bulbs that hung from the railing? How would she track down a drop in the middle of the night, in that cold, along those dark flights of stairs?

In the following days, family by family, word slowly got out, and now everyone in the house knows about it, even if they prefer not to discuss it, as if it were some silly thing that should perhaps embarrass them. Now many ears are strained, in the dark, when night comes to oppress mankind. And some think of one thing, some of another.

Some nights the drop is silent. But other times it does nothing but move for hours on end, up, up, it seems like it might never stop. Our hearts pound whenever its tender footstep seems to reach the ceiling. Thank goodness, it hasn't stopped. There it goes, tick, tick, heading to the floor above.

I'm certain that the tenants of the mezzanine floor think they're safe at this point. The drop — they believe — has already passed by their door and won't have another chance to disturb them; others, like me for example, who live on the sixth floor now have cause to be anxious instead. But who is to say that, in the nights to come, the drop will resume its journey from the point it reached the last time, instead of starting over, beginning its voyage from the first steps, ever damp and dark with abandoned rubbish? No, not even they can feel completely safe.

In the morning, leaving the house, we look carefully at the staircase to see if any trace remains. Nothing, as expected, not even the smallest imprint. After all, who takes this story seriously in the morning? In the morning sun man is strong, he's a lion, even if he was aghast hours earlier.

Or could the people on the mezzanine be right? After all, we — who didn't hear anything at first and considered ourselves spared — even we hear something some nights. The drop is still far away, it's true. Only a very light ticking, a feeble echo through the walls, reaches us. But it's a sign that the thing is climbing, getting ever closer.

It doesn't even help to sleep in an inner room far from the stairwell. Better to hear the noise, rather than spending the nights in doubt over whether it's there or not. Sometimes those who live in those rooms can't resist; they sneak silently into the hallways and stand in the foyer in the freezing cold, behind the door, listening with bated breath. If they hear *it*, they don't dare walk away; they are slaves to incomprehensible fears. Worse, though, if everything is quiet, then how can they be sure that the noise won't begin as soon as they've gone back to bed?

What a strange life. And not to be able to complain, or try to remedy it, or find an explanation to soothe the soul. And not even to be able to persuade others, from other

houses, who don't know. But what can this drop be — they ask in exasperatingly good faith — maybe a mouse? A little toad escaped from the cellar? No.
And so — they insist — could it perhaps be an allegory? If you like, you could say it symbolizes death? Or some danger? Or the passing of the years? Not at all, folks: it's simply a drop. It's just that it's going up the stairs.

Or, more subtly, is it meant to represent dreams and delusions? Longed-for, faraway lands where we assume we'd be happy? Something poetic, in short? No, absolutely not. Or else the places even farther out, at the edge of the world, the ones we'll never reach? But no, I'm telling you, it's not a joke, there are no double meanings but, alas, just a drop of water, as far as we can tell, that goes up the stairs at night. Tick, tick, mysteriously, step by step. And that's why we're afraid.

BARE IN MIND

HILARY LEICHTER

Eleanor invited us over to help her go minimalist. "I'm cleaning house!" she said. We arrived at her apartment with large, shiny bags from the home goods store, and smaller, shiny bags from the grocery store. The plan was to fill our bags to the brim with Eleanor's things, and then haul the bags back to our bedrooms and kitchens and possess the unassuming objects until they transitioned into objects of our own, until they bored us, until we also decided to go minimalist and force the possessions on someone else. This was a ritual we called a "swap," or a "giveaway," or a "gutting," or a "Here, you take this, this looks so nice on you, this looks so much better on you than it does on me." The complicated provenance of our stuff.

But Eleanor's apartment was practically empty, as vacant as a model home. Nothing save a mattress, two hats hanging from hooks, a table and chairs pushed against the far windowed wall. Our shiny bags floated on the freshly swept floors like the crumpled trash of giants.

"We thought you were decluttering?" "Yes," Eleanor said. "Decluttering *here*," and she pointed to her head. Eleanor liked to try new things. She was the first of us to take a trapeze class, and so this was just another acrobatic development. She lifted the hats from their hooks, and gave one of the hats to us. We passed it back and forth among ourselves, familiar with the idea of hats, but not in this context. Eleanor put on the second hat herself, and motioned for us to follow her into the apartment.

To start, Eleanor gave away a favorite anecdote about bug repellant. It went through one hat and straight over to the other. Next, she passed along a recipe for corn fritters. "I never cook these days," Eleanor laughed. "I've sold my pots and pans!"

She uploaded the story of her education into the brim of the fedora, and it made its way through the straw cap sitting on Yuki's head. "I didn't know you studied semiotics," Yuki said, and Eleanor looked at her blankly. "I did?" Then Eleanor had to give this knowledge back to Yuki, again, to prevent her brain from refilling itself.

We traded turns wearing the hat, receiving Eleanor's refuse in shifts. Eleanor had a lot of great ideas, and a lot of lousy ones, too. Her head was like any closet, its contents both worthless and priceless in equal measure. She had an encyclopedic knowledge of hair products. She had watched more television than she cared to admit, and lied about the same things we lied about, like her availability the weekend of Brandon's wedding. She was more racist than we had imagined, and less neurotic. She actually read the articles Katja forwarded every week, even the long ones, and not just the headlines. There was a whole business with a pack of monsters dressed as bears, hiding behind an armoire. There was Eleanor's very first thought, an idea about the light that bathed the knotty fibers of her furry, soft pillow. She gave away her ability to sew and her ability to lift weights safely and effectively. Eleanor didn't give Brandon her virginity, but she gave him her memory of losing it.

"I don't understand," Brandon sighed. The day was slinking off toward evening, and Brandon had missed brunch. "Why would you want to make yourself stupid?"
"Not stupid," Eleanor said. "Just empty. I'm making room."

And then, Eleanor put on the fedora, and gave away her idea for going minimalist in the first place. When we left her apartment, we left her with one thought in her head, and nothing else. We walked home with our empty bags. We wanted to know what it was, this shiny final thing, but she wouldn't have told us, even if we had dared to ask. After all, she no longer even knew our names. She chased us down the hallway, screaming like someone we had never met.

Our own heads grew cluttered and heavy. Painful things, happy things, complicated nests of story. The years were tangled with other years. We tried on hats in fashion stores and waited for the thoughts to trickle from our ears, out and out forever. Every now and then we prepared a corn fritter. Every now and then we knew more about a hair product than we felt we should. We kept ourselves cozy with the clutter of well-stocked pantries.

On the long walk up the stairs, on the long drive to the country, on the marathon for retired Olympians, on the trips home from the doctor, on the stroll down the beach, we remembered Eleanor. We pictured her sitting on that bench, in that room, in the passenger seat, one car over. Look at how she points her chin forward into the coming day, we thought. So self-possessed, so single minded.

GENIUS AND DAEMON

A.E. STALLINGS

The MacArthur Foundation discourages journalists from referring to its generous fellowships as "genius" grants, but if you are lucky enough to have been awarded one of these (the phone call astonishes out of the blue), the label seems inevitable. Sooner or later, someone will call you a genius, and not necessarily in a nice way. Maybe it will be sarcastic. Even uttered affectionately, it tends to be with a dash of irony, as when your husband points out the glasses you are searching for are on top of your head. Almost never does anyone use it to mean: "You are unutterably brilliant." And it isn't a helpful word to have in mind as you sit down to the blank page. Once you feel that your poems must be works of genius, it can be hard to commit a poem at all. Is this genius? What about *this*? Writer's block peers from a corner of the room, rubbing its long, thin hands like a fly.

So maybe you start to think about the word itself. Our word genius comes from the Latin, where it is related to the word for coming into being (think "generation"). A genius was a spirit associated with a person, a family (consider William Carlos Williams as the "happy genius" of his household in "Danse Russe"), or even a place (a *genius loci*). The genius of a place was often represented — in art and literature — as an autochthonous snake. (D. H. Lawrence's "Snake" seems to be one of these, a "lord of life.") A person acquired their genius at birth; a great man obviously had a great genius. (Strictly speaking, a woman did not have a "genius," but a "juno." Perhaps a woman with a MacArthur fellowship has a "juno grant.") In the cults to emperors, originally the sacrifices were not made to the emperor himself, but to his genius. Our "genius" has retained this positive spin, as well as the notion that genius is something that one is born with, not something that can be honed or acquired; begotten, not made.

"Genius" is also, though, how Latin translated the Greek word "Daimon," a word that has been, well, demonized in Christianity, where it now only refers to an evil spirit. "Daemon" shows up in both Homer and Hesiod. In Homer, a daemon was simply an unspecified deity. When Menelaus in the *Odyssey* tactfully wants to absolve Helen for risky behavior that nearly exposes the Greeks (including himself) hiding in the Trojan horse, he says that a *daemon* made her do it. The etymology of "daemon" associates it with division and allotment — daemons were the apportioners of men's fates. Heraclitus for example, said that man's character is his *daemon* — usually translated as "fate." Hesiod (maybe late eighth century BC), who, the ancients thought, predated Homer, had a more specific theology of daemons. According to Hesiod, the men of the good and just Golden Age continued to walk the earth as spirits after their race had perished. "Thrice myriad," or 30,000 of them, which is Hesiodic shorthand for "a lot," continue according to him to move among us cloaked in invisibility, observing the behavior of men and reporting directly to Zeus on crimes and injustice; they also hold the key to prosperity.

It seems to be Socrates (fifth century BC) who eventually personalizes the daemon. Socrates (or Plato voicing Socrates) often tweaks the proto-theology of Hesiod. Playfully, for instance, he tells a story that the cicadas had once been men, but on the discovery of music, quit eating and drinking in their intoxication, and shriveled up into chirring insects. But, like Hesiod's daemons, they remain on earth, and report to the Muses on human misbehavior in the arts, for a bad rhyme or bumpy scansion, say, or singing out of tune. Socrates claimed that he had a personal daemonic something — a voice — that spoke to him, often as a warning, and which he obeyed. Socrates also gives us a view of poetic inspiration that is similar to that of the Romantics — poets produce their poems not out of craft or effort, but under the effects of inspiration, or, in Greek, *enthusiasm* (god-possessed), the ecstasy of being taken over by a higher power (the Muses). This thrill was transferred through the poet to the audience by a mysterious force akin to magnetism.

The Romantic notion of the poet, not far from the Socratic one, is in fact often associated with "demonic" genius — again, a kind of possession, beyond the poet's control. (A poet, like Byron, might be "mad, bad, and dangerous to know.") With the current professionalization of poetry, MFA programs and conferences, the emphasis on "workshops" — a word out of carpentry, or art-as-factory — that dangerous glamour of genius is, perhaps, helpfully less prevalent. Does anyone anymore think a poem springs onto the page without revisions and drafts, conceived in a hectic fever?

Yet most poets, I think, do experience from time to time something they would call inspiration, when a poem is greater than the sum of its parts, when it means more than you thought it did, when a new image or sound surprises you, when you wonder, where did that come from? The Canadian poet Mark Strand, with whom I taught a seminar in Sewanee, Tennessee, for two summers, would say that his poems were smarter than he was. When I teach aspiring poets, I try to get them away from trying to make a poem be a mouthpiece for something they want to say. You shouldn't be telling the poem what to do, I tell them; the poem is trying to tell *you* something. Or maybe what I mean is, rather than worry about demonstrating your genius, listen to your daemon.

VIVIAN MAIER CONSIDERS HEAVEN FROM A BENCH IN ROGERS BEACH PARK CHICAGO

SHANE MCCRAE

In heaven nobody will be alone
In heaven   except for me and nobody
        Nobody calls   nobody comes
My nobody expands across the country

The way a parachute expands across
The sky   it does if you're right under it
        In heaven they'll throw me   in the lost
And found   where I guess everybody goes

At first   now   that I think about it   what
Will be my special place apart   I wonder
        Or will they leave me in the lost
And found box after they have scooped the heaven-

ly out   a permanent person in a temporary place   roles are reversed in heaven
        Nobody calls   nobody comes
In heaven I expect the children are

A kind of furniture   nobody sits on
Like flowers in Manhattan   maybe sometimes
        They're brought to God and God says *This one*
And that   ottoman is sent back to life

A baby   and for some this seems to never
Happen   I think I'm such a child returned
        Most things in my life seemed to never
Happen before they happened   now they seem to

Have never happened though they have   for the time
Being I am   for now I'm stuck in most
        Things having never happened I'm
A lamp   shining in an abandoned building

But for a lamp I think that would be heaven

CONTRIBUTORS

Dr. Joshua Bennett hails from Yonkers, New York. He is the author of *The Sobbing School* (Penguin, 2016) and *Being Property Once Myself: Blackness and the End of Man*, (Harvard University Press). Bennett holds a PhD in English from Princeton University, and an MA in Theatre and Performance Studies from the University of Warwick, where he was a Marshall Scholar. His writing has appeared or is forthcoming in *The American Poetry Review*, *The New York Times*, the *Paris Review*, *Poetry*, and elsewhere. He is currently a Junior Fellow in the Society of Fellows at Harvard University.

Venita Blackburn's work has appeared in *American Short Fiction*, the *Georgia Review*, *Pleiades*, *Madison Review*, *Bat City Review*, *Nashville Review*, *Smoke Long Quarterly*, *Café Irreal*, *Santa Monica Review*, *Faultline*, *Devil's Lake Review*, *Nat.Brut.*, *Bellevue Literary Review*, audio download through Bound Off, and others. Her collection of short stories, *Black Jesus and Other Superheroes*, was published 2017. She earned her MFA from Arizona State University in 2008, and is finishing a new novel, *Babel*, and a collection of flash fiction and nonfiction. Her home town is Compton, California, and she will join the MFA faculty of California State University, Fresno, in the fall of 2018.

Dino Buzzati (1906–1972) was an Italian writer, painter, journalist, and playwright. Buzzati spent much of his career as a critic and reporter for the *Corriere della Sera*. He is the author of the novel *The Tartar Steppe*, *Poem Strip*, which he wrote and illustrated in 1969, has been called the first Italian graphic novel. He was a prolific author of short fiction, of hundreds of stories inflected by reportage or verging on prose poetry. Translated by: **Zoë Slutzky**, a writer and translator in New York. She is a PhD candidate in comparative literature at the Graduate Center (City University of New York), and teaches literature at Hunter College.

Sloane Crosley is the author of *The New York Times* bestselling essay collections, *I Was Told There'd Be Cake*, *How Did You Get This Number* and the novel *The Clasp*. She served as editor of *The Best American Travel Writing* series and is featured in The Library of America's *50 Funniest American Writers* as well as *The Best American Nonrequired Reading*. Her new book of essays is *Look Alive Out There*.

Helen DeWitt is the author of *The Last Samurai* and *Lightning Rods*. *Some Trick*, her first collection of stories, will be published by New Directions in May 2018.

Johanna Drucker is the inaugural Breslauer Professor of Bibliographical Studies in the Department of Information Studies at UCLA. Her most recent books are *The General Theory of Social Relativity* and the eco-novel, *Downdrift*.

Jorie Graham is the author, most recently, of *Fast* and *From The New World (Poems 1976–2014)*. She lives in Massachusetts and teaches at Harvard.

Rachel Hadas is the author of many books of poetry, essays, and translations. Her most recent poetry collection is *Questions in the Vestibule* (Northwestern University Press 2016); her verse translations of Euripides' two Iphigenia plays are forthcoming this spring, also fron Northwestern. *Poems for Camilla*, a new collection, is due out in summer 2019 from Measure Press.

Anosh Irani has published four critically acclaimed novels: *The Cripple and His Talismans*, *The Song of Kahunsha*, *Dahanu Road*, and *The Parcel*. He is also the author of the *Bombay Black* and the anthology *The Bombay Plays: The Matka King & Bombay Black*. His most recent play is *The Men in White*. His work has been translated into 11 languages.

Sara Jaffe is a fiction writer living in Portland, Oregon. Her novel *Dryland* was published by Tin House Books in 2015. Her short fiction and criticism have appeared or are upcoming in publications including *Catapult*, *Fence*, *BOMB*, *NOON*, and *The Offing*. She co-edited *The Art of Touring* (Yeti, 2009), an anthology of writing and visual art by musicians drawing on her experience as guitarist for post-punk band Erase Errata. She is currently working on a collection of short fiction entitled *Hurricane Envy*.

Jac Jemc is most recently the author of *The Grip of It* (FSG Originals). Her first novel, *My Only Wife* (Dzanc Books) was a finalist for the 2013 PEN/Robert W. Bingham Prize for Debut Fiction and winner of the Paula Anderson Book Award, and her collection of stories, *A Different Bed Every Time* (Dzanc Books) was named one of Amazon's best story collections of 2014. She edits nonfiction for Hobart.

Zeynep Kayhan lives in Maçka, Istanbul.

Paul LaFarge is the author of the novels *The Night Ocean*, *The Artist of the Missing*, *Haussmann, or the Distinction,* and *Luminous Airplanes*; and a book of imaginary dreams, *The Facts of Winter*. His stories and nonfiction have appeared in *The New Yorker*, *The New Republic*, *The Paris Review*, *Harper's*, and elsewhere.

Hilary Leichter's work has been published in *The New Yorker*, *n+1*, *American Short Fiction*, *The Southern Review*, *BOMB Magazine*, *The Rumpus*, *Tin House*, and elsewhere. She teaches creative writing at Columbia University.

Massimo Mazzotti is a professor in the History of Science at UC Berkeley and director of its Center for Science, Technology, Medicine and Society. He is the author of *The World of Maria Gaetana Agnesi, Mathematician of God* (2007).

Shane McCrae is the author of *In the Language of My Captor* (Wesleyan University Press, 2017), which was a finalist for the National Book Award, and four previous books. His poems have appeared in the *Best American Poetry* series, *Poetry*, *The American Poetry Review*, *Gulf Coast*, and other anthologies and journals. He teaches at Columbia University, and lives in New York City.

Yxta Maya Murray is a writer and a law professor who lives in Los Angeles.

Aaron Robertson is a James Reston Reporting Fellow for *The New York Times.* He has written for *The Nation*, *Detroit Metro Times*, *The Point Magazine*, and more. He is currently completing an MSt in Modern Languages at the University of Oxford.

Isaac Bashevis Singer (1903-1991) was a Polish-born Yiddish-American author of short stories, novels, memoirs, and stories for children. Among the many awards he received was the Nobel Prize for Literature. Translated by **David Stromberg**, a writer, translator, and literary scholar based in Jerusalem.

A.E. Stallings is an American poet and translator who has lived in Greece since 1999. Her new translation of Hesiod's *Works and Days* is recently out from Penguin Classics, and a new book of poems is forthcoming this autumn from Farrar, Straus and Giroux.

Scott Timberg is the editor of *The Misread City: New Literary Los Angeles* and author of *Culture Crash: The Killing of the Creative Class*, an examination of the damages to our cultural landscape wrought by recent technological and economic shifts and an argument for a more equitable and navigable future.

Sally Wen Mao is the author of *Mad Honey Symposium* (Alice James Books, 2014). Her second book, *Oculus*, is forthcoming from Graywolf Press in 2019. Her work has won a 2017 Pushcart Prize and is published or forthcoming in *A Public Space*, *Poetry*, *Black Warrior Review*, *Guernica*, *The Missouri Review*, *Tin House*, *The Best of the Net 2014*, and *The Best American Poetry 2013*, among others. Mao is currently the 2017–2018 Jenny McKean Moore Writer in Washington at the George Washington University.

David Yezzi's most recent books of poems are *Birds of the Air* and *Black Sea*, both from Carnegie Mellon. His verse play *Schnauzer* is forthcoming later this year from Exot Books. He is chair of the Writing Seminars at Johns Hopkins and editor of *The Hopkins Review.*

FEATURED ARTISTS

Jaap Blonk (b. 1953, Woerden, Netherlands) is a self-taught composer and poet. His unfinished studies in mathematics and musicology inspired work in the Dada vein. In the early 1980s, he discovered the power and flexibility of his voice, and set out on a long-term exploration of phonetics and the possibilities of the human voice. Blonk now specializes in sound poetry, performing and giving workshops worldwide. With the use of live electronics, the scope and range of his work has grown considerably. His sound poetry scores are an independent body of visual work, which has been widely published and exhibited.

Luchita Hurtado (b. 1920, Maiquetía, Venezuela), is a Los Angeles-based artist. Hurtado began her career as a fashion illustrator for Condé Nast and a muralist for Lord & Taylor, and she fell into an artistic scene that included Isamu Noguchi, Wilfredo Lam, Man Ray, and Rufino Tamayo, among others. Hurtado married the Austrian artist Wolfgang Paalen in 1945, and traveling between New York and Mexico City, her personal and artistic activity centered on the post-Surrealist Dyn group who sought to break away from André Breton and the Surrealists, seeking a new aesthetic and cultural order that looked to ancient Mesoamerican culture as its guide with its premodern blend of art, science, and religion.

Kerry James Marshall (b. 1955, Birmingham, Alabama) is an American artist born in Birmingham, Alabama. He studied at the Otis Art Institute in Los Angeles, earning his B.F.A. in 1978 and an honorary doctorate in 1999. He is well known for his paintings depicting actual and imagined events from African-American history. In 2017, the Museum of Contemporary Art in Los Angeles presented *Kerry James Marshall: Mastry*, the first major museum survey of the artist's work.

Gala Porras-Kim (b. 1984, Bogotá, Colombia; lives and works in Los Angeles) received an MFA from the California Institute of the Arts and an MA in Latin American Studies from the University of California, Los Angeles. Forthcoming exhibitions will be held at the Seoul National Museum of Art; the Headlands Center for the Arts; and the Bowdoin College Museum of Art. Recent exhibitions include: *Journal d'un travailleur métèque du futur*, FRAC Pays de la Loire, France; *Made in L.A. 2016: a, the, though, only,* Hammer Museum, LA, CA; *Current LA,* Los Angeles Public Art Biennial; *Aún*, 44th National Salon of Artists, Bogotá, Colombia; *For Prospective Rock/Artifact Projection*, The Bindery Projects, Minneapolis, MN; and *Prospecting Notes About Sounds*, 18th Street Arts Center. Porras-Kim's work is included in *A Universal History of Infamy*, LACMA, Pacific Standard Time: LA/LA.

Brian Randolph (b. 1979) lives and works in Los Angeles. His work has been included in group exhibitions at BBQ LA, (Los Angeles), Ms. Barber's (Los Angeles), and Spring Break Art Show (New York), and in solo exhibitions at Odd Ark LA (Los Angeles), School 33 Art Center (Baltimore) and Gallery 4 (Baltimore). Brian received a BFA from the Maryland Institute College of Art in 2001.

Rodrigo Valenzuela (b. 1982, Santiago, Chile) recently joined the Department of Art faculty, UCLA. He received an art history degree from the U. of Chile in 2004. He worked in construction while completing an MFA at the U. of Washington. Using staged scenes and digital interventions, Valenzuela's work is rooted in documentary and fiction, often involving narratives around immigration and the working class.

Genius is the instinct for
knowing when to stop.
– John Butler Yeats